21798

*Catholicism*
*Confronts*
*Modernity*

# CATHOLICISM CONFRONTS MODERNITY

*A Protestant View*

## LANGDON GILKEY

*A Crossroad Book*

The Seabury Press · New York

The Seabury Press
815 Second Avenue
New York, N.Y. 10017

LIBRARY OF CONGRESS CATALOGING IN PUBLICATION DATA

Gilkey, Langdon, 1919–
    Catholicism confronts modernity.

    "A Crossroad book."
    1. Catholic Church.  2.  Modernism—Catholic
Church.  3.  Catholic Church History—20th century.
I.  Title.
BX1396.G54        282′.09′047        74-19167
ISBN 0-8164-1163-8

for
MARY JANE

# *Preface*

These chapters on Catholicism and the spirit of modernity have grown out of lectures and addresses I have given to Catholic audiences over the past six years, in each of which some aspect of the encounter of these forces has been interpreted. Although I am not a Catholic theologian, I have always been welcomed, not only with the greatest courtesy, but even more as a fellow communicant and friend. I wish to thank the members of those groups and also the many Catholic theological students whose presence, since 1965, has graced the University of Chicago Divinity School and with whom I have had the privilege of extended serious and frank discussion of many of the matters that I take up in this book. Finally, I wish especially to thank my friend and colleague in systematic theology, Professor David Tracy, with whom all of this has been thrashed out over and over again, and who, along with Professor Jerald Bruaer, was kind enough to read chapter I and to suggest needed amendments. It was Father Tracy who first suggested that I seek to publish my interpretation of the present Catholic crisis, even though, needless to say, he is by no means responsible either for the mistakes or for any of the deviant notions that may be contained in this volume.

I have dedicated this book, in lifelong affection, to my sister, Mary Jane Gilkey.

LANGDON GILKEY

*The University of Chicago*
March 1, 1974

# Contents

*Catholicism*
*Confronts*
*Modernity*

# Chapter I

## *The Nature of the Crisis*

FOR A PROTESTANT theologian to publish a book centering on the "crisis" in Catholicism is an unusual, not to say presumptuous, enterprise. "What does he know about it?"; "What right has he to speak on this?"; and "Of what possible interest are his views?" are questions that will naturally leap into the reader's mind. Right at the start, therefore, some explanation of this presumption is in order.

First of all, while I am and shall remain a Protestant Christian, I find in myself, at first to my own surprise, a steadily growing interest in and respect for the Catholic tradition, for the Catholic church herself, and above all, as we grow ever closer in theological, academic, and personal fellowship, for Catholic people. Even more, as a Christian I find in myself an increased concern for the spiritual strength and the institutional health of the Catholic church. More important, however, is my belief that interested Protestants, despite their obvious (and perhaps painful) ignorance of the details of Catholic tradition and of the fine points of current discussions among Catholics, may nevertheless have something useful to say to Catholics about "their" crisis. The reasons for this belief are twofold: the crisis has arisen in large part because of the deep effects of modernity on the Catholic church—a belief I shall seek to justify in all that follows; and Protestantism has for approximately two centuries both sought and been compelled to deal with the same developing modernity, sometimes creatively and sometimes unsuccessfully. Whereas the Catholic crisis has been recent and very sudden, "ours" has been long and drawn out. Thereby, in contemplating their own history, Protestants have had ample opportunity to see the anatomy of this developing interaction of modernity and Christianity: the factors in modernity that have caused the crisis, as well as a very great deal that is creative in modern Protestantism, and the varied effects that these factors have had on our own spiritual and institutional life. Consequently, Protestants *may* be able to help Catholics to diagnose their ills, and to understand what has suddenly happened to them, because much the same has happened over so long a time to us. For this reason, and this alone—not because he can help resolve or answer these problems in a "Catholic" way—a Protestant may presume to analyze what the nature of the crisis in Catholicism is.

To those both within and without her massive walls, present-day Roman Catholicism presents a scene of vast, almost unrelieved confusion. Suddenly, almost in the twinkling of an eye, this seemingly changeless and unified institution, a veritable fortress impervious to outside assault, untroubled by visible or at least dangerous internal dissension, and slowly growing anew in influence and power where for two hundred years she had been weak,[1] finds herself subject to convulsive and cumulative changes. Many of her fundamental practices have slipped away; her most cherished dogmas and sacrosanct authorities are scorned by many and ignored or questioned by most; her formerly changeless patterns of life are altered by an accelerating flux of fads; and her treasured unity is broken by intense inner conflicts.[2] None of the changeless structures on which conservative defenders of the old order depended appears now either safe or stable; alternatively, any new "health" that liberals hoped would come from reforms of those structures seems in this present confusion to be more hidden than manifest. If she tries to remain a conservative, and thus changeless, fortress, Catholicism seems destined to lose her clerical and lay leadership; if she continues to adjust to the world in increasingly liberal reforms, it seems questionable that any recognizable institutional structure of a Catholic sort will long remain. How to retain at once both her Catholic structure and her leadership seems to be not so much a question as an unresolvable dilemma.

Thus the *aggiornamento*, which the conservatives feared might weaken, and which liberals believed would rejuvenate and so strengthen the church, seems in fact to have endangered her very life. This is above all evident in the well-documented facts that clergy are not only leaving their vocations in increasing numbers, but dangerously few new ones are appearing to take their places; and that many former liberals, both lay and clerical, have, after a decade of battles over innovations, lost their "ultimate concern" for church, religion, or God and have left the Christian community entirely and without regret.[3] Every traditional, secure, changeless foundation guarding her past forms of institutional and religious life—dogma, theology, authority, canon law, practice—has been rudely shaken if not yet toppled. No corresponding modern foundations or structures have appeared with authentic power to replace them. Thus does the Roman church, as a social institution, as a form of piety or religious life, and as a form of faith or theology, seem to many within Catholicism to be weak and vulnerable in the extreme,[4] crumbling in disintegration like ancient Rome herself. And to some conservative Catholic observers this disintegration of the Roman citadel has proceeded for reasons parallel to those that, according to Gibbon, once dismantled Imperial Rome: liberal priests within (like their Christian forefathers in Imperial Rome) have so weakened her traditional defenses that the church is now unable as before to withstand the forces of barbaric modernity assaulting her from without.

Periods of institutional, intellectual, and spiritual crisis are not, however, necessarily barren and uncreative in their outcome. Any student of secular history—or of the history of the biblical covenant with Israel—knows that the most important creative moments of history, secular or religious, arise when the foundations of an old order have been shaken so that a new birth can take place. Possibly the divine promise to be "with the church for all time" is not a promise to protect her from such rude shaking in history or to preserve in a static changelessness her traditional forms of institutional structure and of dogmatic theology. The shaking has occurred, it now seems evident, precisely because of the anachronistic nature of her structures and the now apparent relativity of her traditional viewpoints. It was a quite *different* promise that founded the *ecclesia*, namely the promise to provide the grace to create *new* forms of life in each successive age, forms more capable than the older ones of ministering authentically to each new age. It is with that hope in mind, and from the viewpoint of that interpretation of both the divine promise and of the crisis in Roman Catholicism, that these chapters have been written.

The Catholic crisis opens up many theological questions fundamental for every Christian: the relation of basic *changes* in cultural life to the church and to her theology, and to her forms of authority, piety, and daily life; the relation of the *collapse* of traditional structures of social and church life to the rise of *new* structures; and the relation of these changes in history to the divine *promises* and the divine *activity* that give to a moving and shifting history its meaning and its hope. In surveying the present Roman scene, we find ourselves pondering the paradox of the relativity and yet the absoluteness of Christian faith in a world of radical historical becoming; and how this simultaneous relativity and yet this absoluteness are to be understood in relation to change, to each other, and to the future. For on the one hand, in this crisis a whole Catholic Christian generation has to its dismay and with genuine suffering experienced the radicality of historical *change*; such change engulfs and relativizes each historical embodiment, even the ecclesial embodiments of the faith that transcends history. On the other hand, any *Christian* contemplation of the shifting course of history that so continually relativizes and engulfs every apparently stable form of institution, discovers it to be a history whose meaning and hope are not engulfed by change. Rather, that meaning and hope find their grounds beyond that change, and ahead of it, in the divine will which is both the source of our creativity and the mysterious origin of the destruction out of which creativity continually arises.

Change is the basic reality of history; it is in some way the character of whatever being there is. The flux of becoming, not the changelessness of being, characterizes our existence and that of our world. All is in process through time, and nothing stands still. This profound intuition of modernity—the historicity of nature, of man and his institutions—has been deeply felt by us all with regard to our *secular* institutions: political, economic, and social, are now seen, not as eternal orders established by God, but as historical structures created by historical destiny and human creativity, and thus continually subject to transformation. Modern living, because of industrialism and technology, has accelerated and deepened this experience of a changing world until coping with change, being serene in its midst, comprehending its causes and anatomy, and guiding it creatively into humane channels, have become the leading political, economic, and social challenges of our time. Our forms of communal life—in property, economic structure, politics and government, education, personal values and goals—cannot possibly retain their health and usefulness if they remain precisely what they were in the different world of the nineteenth century. Historical change thus forces us to creative re-evaluation, reinterpretation, and reformulation. It requires a balance of courage and indefatigable hope if any communal "way of life" is at once to be freely and openly changed and yet to retain its best and most fundamental values. This deep experience of historical change, with its terrors and its possibilities, its challenges for reinterpretation and reformulation of what was thought to be changeless, has now been experienced in Catholicism in the even deeper area of religious life, in matters of "ultimate concern" (which has for two hundred and fifty years been felt in secular affairs) and with all the same confusion, terrors, challenges, and possibilities.

In such a situation of deep ecclesiastical change several things are required:

1. The major *reflective* requirement for creatively dealing with such radical change is to understand the causes and anatomy of the process, and thereby the *possibilities* for valid re-evaluation, reinterpretation, and reformulation of traditional symbols and structures so that they may live again.[5] Creative historical action in the face of change demands praxis, practical work for the future guided by *theory* or *understanding* both of the concrete structure of change and of the goals to be achieved in the future: an open discussion of what has happened to Catholicism and why is indispensable, and of what is appropriate in the new world that change has brought to us.

2. The major *political* requirement essential to dealing with such change is to direct the process so as to remain loyal to the deepest levels of tradition and yet also to be

open to experiment with new and creative forms. In this
sense it necessitates some reasoned understanding of what
authentic Catholicism *is* in order to realize legitimate
goals for the immediate future. Again, an open discussion
of the fundamentals of Catholic life and faith is necessary
in the light of this onslaught of change.

3. The major *spiritual* requirement is to be balanced
and open, serene and confident, amidst the anxieties, even
the terrors, of this experience of radical change in structures that previously have borne our security in time. This
is a tremendous demand whether in secular or in ecclesiastical life. With regard to the *ecclesia* it requires in turn
a reinterpretation, not only of the relation of emerging
Catholicism to former forms of Catholic life, but also of
the way God works within historical processes, both secular and ecclesiastical. The fact of Catholic change requires a reinterpretation of Catholic theology of history.

The present crisis of Catholicism is, then, one of the
most valid contemporary events in which to view, in all
their mystery and terror, the ambiguity and the promise
of our human situation: the convulsion and shattering of
the old, treasured forms, the threats of consequent decay
and dissolution, the recognition that ultimacy and meaning reside in history solely within structures that are relative and transient, and yet the continual promise of the
new as older forms pass away. For here in the Catholic
crisis is manifested the relativity and vulnerability of
what seems most essential and permanent in history, the
mutability of what is most eternal, the possible death of
what must be most alive. How are these themes of
change, decay, and the promise of the new, long evident
in secular social history, now to be understood in relation
to the *ecclesia*, in relation to "sacred" as well as to "profane" history?[6] To understand this event as at once the
work of historical relativity and change, and yet at the
same time as the result of the creative providence of God,

is to understand better history and church alike, and their relation to God's grace. The event itself, as well as the pressures of modernity that have brought it about, forces on us all a fundamental theological reformulation of the meaning of the *ecclesia* in relation to the changing forms of history, and so finally a reinterpretation of the meaning of the divine activity in history and of the divine promise for the future.

The work of God in history has often been assumed to be embodied in institutional forms, which were as a consequence necessarily changeless. If they were in truth "divine," they were, like God, eternal, everlasting and beyond relativity, time, and change. Gradually, however, the notion of changeless forms in a changing history, in history itself, in politics, economics, biology, and even in physics and theology, has shifted. In contemporary reflection God is seen to work *through* changing forms. Correspondingly, grace or the divine quality is evident in historical change not so much in the stability of forms as in the direction of the change of forms; it is manifest in the spirit that animates their progressive realization, and in the love, commitment, and mission that result from each historical embodiment; and grace is realized in the goal toward which this process of change moves. The "sacrality" of the *ecclesia* is not found in the changelessness of her forms, but in her fidelity through changing forms to her mission in the world and so to the final purpose of God.

What is, therefore, continuous in this process of changing forms can be neither the precise form of her dogmas and doctrines, her institutional and hierarchical structures, her codes of law, nor the shape of her liturgy and daily practices. For these are precisely what *are* subject to change. Rather, the continuous, besides the presence of the divine Spirit and its human correlates of faith, hope and love, is expressed in the common symbols around which this communal life in history fashions itself: these symbols express the ground of her life in the divine activity and the goal of her life in the divine purpose. Such essential symbols provide the basis for the beliefs and reflection of the community, its modes of worship and behavior, its social and political forms of life, its ethical decisions, and the shape of its mission. And such symbols must be continuously reinterpreted and re-expressed; they must be embodied in ever new and more creative institutional forms; and they must result in new understanding of the mission and work of the church in the world.

Ironically, precisely this new view of the depth and all-pervasiveness of historical change and of the relativity of all forms within a meaningful process has precipitated the crisis of traditional Catholic forms of religious life. Possibly this view, which is in fact very close to the biblical understanding of God's relation to history, people and covenant alike, may prove the basis in reflection for the needed reinterpretation and reformulation of Catholic existence.

The crisis of Catholicism is important not merely as an illustration of the mystery of the relative and the absolute in history, but because it provides the historical occasion and the ecclesiastical locus for what is creatively new to arise in Christianity in our time. As the *crisis* character of this situation reveals—and Protestantism in a less intense way manifests the same problems—no form of spiritual life can be alien to its time and to the cultural life of that time. What is called for desperately throughout the Christian churches is a synthesis of Christian revelation and modernity, of the Christian witness and life with the forms of our age, a synthesis with power and authenticity, and thus one as authentically true to the gospel as it is relevant to modernity. The only alternatives are to assert either that some traditional synthesis created in the historical past—be it that of the fourth, the thirteenth, or the sixteenth centuries—was such to be eternally valid for subsequent ages; or that modernity is so estranged from God that no authentic synthesis is now possible and that past forms of authenticity, even if now irrelevant to many, remain our only option. The first of these assertions denies the relativity of all things historical, and the second denies the universality over time as well as over space of the divine providence and grace. If such a twentieth-century synthesis creating a powerful and authentic form of Christianity is to be expected, it will arise, despite the visible chaos within her present life, from within Roman Catholicism rather than elsewhere in the Christian world.

Some characteristics of such a creative synthesis I shall outline in the chapters that follow. I mean to reinterpret, rethink, and reappropriate the traditional symbols of our Christian tradition in the terms of modern experience. These symbols will be reinterpreted with the experiential content of modern modes of experiencing self, others, and the world, with the modern conceptual forms of seeing and understanding the world, and with institutional structures in touch with our own understanding of divine authority and of human autonomy. The presuppositions about man's life and religion, God, and the meaning of Christian symbols, will become clearer as we proceed. Here I only need to say that this view is based on the conviction that the divine that we call God supports, undergirds, judges, and heals our entire existence in the world, inward and outward, individual and social. Faith is the specific awareness of that continuing presence, dependence on it, commitment to its call and the mission that call entails, repentance in the face of its judgments, acceptance of its acceptance of us, and hope for the future in its power, goodness, and love. Christian faith, then, is a conscious awareness of and a committed relation to this continuous and healing divine presence of God the Father

of Jesus Christ, a presence that is experienced, understood, thematized, and so related to and enacted in terms
of the symbols of our Christian tradition.

Religious symbols are the way in which any community, religious or secular, structures the ultimate horizon
in which it lives, and so understands the meaning, the
vocation, and the destiny of its own life in the world.
Christian symbols are the treasured means by which our
community and our tradition, springing from Jesus the
Christ, structures its ultimate horizon and understands
the meaning, mission, and destiny of its life; it is through
these symbols that the community relates to and speaks of
God. I regard these symbols of this tradition as *true*—that
is, as the way of understanding ourselves and our world,
of understanding and relating to God, and so of acting in
our world and for the future, that provides the most adequate and coherent account of human being in the world.
Religious symbols, like all fundamental social symbols,
structure human experience and give that experience coherence, meaning, and healing. By thematizing experiences into understanding and so in part conquering the
terrors to which life is subject, they bring into awareness
those sacral elements of human existence that are cele-
brated in joy, and give creative guidance for action, and
provide intelligible, credible grounds for hope in the future. Religious symbols are effective not in and of themselves alone, as if they were more or less useful "pictures"
or "ideas" with which we paint ourselves and our world.
Rather they are effective as *communicating* the reality in
which we live and on which we depend in our past, present, and future. Symbols are in effect sacraments, visible
and conceptual signs of an inward or transcendent grace
through which alone we may exist.

If this be the character and role of religious symbols, it
is evident that the *content* of these symbolic forms—what
is structured, thematized, and healed—is ordinary and

"natural" human experience, and so the common experience of the men and women who live, worship, and face the future. Contemporary life must provide the experiential content and the conceptual forms of these symbols lest the men and women who seek to live in their terms find them empty, meaningless, and impotent.[7] Thus each age and each cultural "place" must reinterpret its symbolic heritage in the terms of its own life: in terms of its lived experience of self, others, and the world, of the problems and possibilities that emerge out of this world; and of the conceptual forms with which it understands and copes with the realities around it. If the *kerygma*, the gospel, is to speak to our age, it must do so in relation to the moods and forms of modern self-understanding. A positive relation to modernity is essential if contemporary Christianity is to have authenticity and power. As Gregory Baum has said of the church: "She will proclaim the same symbols, but their meaning will be different: they will clarify sin and salvation in the present age. In the new agenda, truth demands the reinterpretation of symbols."[8]

That process of reinterpretation has been carried on in the Protestant communions for almost two hundred years now. The liberal theology of the nineteenth and early twentieth centuries was a deliberate, if possibly too enthusiastic, effort to reinterpret Christian symbols in the terms of nineteenth-century experience and concepts; and in so doing it laid the groundwork for all subsequent modern theology. Twentieth-century neo-orthodox or dialectical theology, conscious of all in the tradition that had been sacrificed in this liberal rapprochement with modernity, sought to recapture the autonomy and independence of Christian revelation and of the spiritual gospel that came through revelation; but it sought to do this in modern terms.

These two movements within Protestantism were immensely creative and even courageous, and all contemporary theology and religious life stands in their debt. For they first of all, in two different stages, assayed this task of fundamental reinterpretation, of achieving a creative synthesis of Christian faith with modernity. From the eighteenth to the twentieth century Protestant theology was the most creative wing of the whole church. For the issues on which these two movements centered are just the issues that challenge modern Catholicism: the relation of Christian truth to science and to the world order that science studies, the relation of biblical and doctrinal history to historical studies, the relation of divine authority and grace to personal autonomy and freedom, the relation of grace to natural goals in life, and, perhaps most important, the relation of the purposes of God and the calling of the church to the political and social developments of the world, of God's promise of salvation to "this-worldly liberation." These fundamental questions were in Protestant liberalism and neo-orthodoxy *first* broached, frankly and openly discussed, and resolved in part in modern terms. Catholic modernism in the nineteenth and early twentieth centuries also sought to deal creatively with these same problems, especially that of personal autonomy; but the silencing of this movement left this job solely in the hands of Protestants. The principal leaders of recent Catholic theology, especially Karl Rahner and Bernard Lonergan, have subsequently sought to achieve the same goal as that of Protestant neo-orthodoxy, i.e., to synthesize *classical* Christian symbols with modern views of the world, man, truth, and the good. However, on every one of these fronts there is no question that it was Protestantism that took the creative lead. If, therefore, Catholicism would understand what sorts of problems it faces, it would be wiser to study with care the difficulties and flounderings of nineteenth-century liberal Protestantism and of twentieth-century neo-orthodoxy, rather than to concentrate solely either on its own tradition, on present "liberal" Catholics, or even on the Protestant Reformation.

Both of these extremely creative movements, however, ultimately encountered serious problems.[9] The result is that at present, while Protestant theology offers two and possibly three creative options, it seems neither to be producing, nor to have the prospect of producing, any powerful synthesis of modernity and the gospel that can support and enhance Christian life for our time.

The reason for this apparent lack of creative potential is not so much the paucity of good theological minds in Protestantism as the evident weakness of present Protestantism as a form of communal church life. Related essentially to the bourgeois middle-class worlds of Europe, Britain, and America, and in the last two to the "Wasp" worlds of small towns and suburbs, Protestantism seems, despite its conservative and neo-conservative theologies of transcendence, to have been so engulfed in that world as merely to reproduce the individualistic, quantitative, moralistic, nonemotional, and in many respects naturalistic, bourgeois world in ecclesiastical form. Its sense of community is weak, or else defined entirely by its middle-class, white parameters; its liturgical life and its experiential potential are almost nonexistent; its experience of the holy in sermon, sacrament, or common prayer is fleeting at best; and its ethical existence is largely an anachronistic individual moralism subscribed to' by all in theory but practiced only by its clerical leaders.[10] The life of Protestant communities seems to me to be either too much a reproduction of the middle-class, suburban world that they serve (as seems the case in America); or, in dogmatically retaining traditional forms of preaching, liturgy, and theology, to be too unrelated to the modes of life, experience, and thought of their society (as seems to me to be the case in Protestant Europe). Only in the pentecostal communities—which Protestantism seems to become when it is not middle-class—in the black churches, in the inner-city experiments, and in some very lively but restricted academic and seminary communities, does Protestantism at the present seem to possess a communal spiritual life strong enough to provide a matrix for such a valid intellectual synthesis; and none of these "fringe" communities to mainline Protestantism are for a variety of intelligible reasons capable of effecting that creative synthesis. This will be a judgment that many will dispute. I feel it is sound; and thus, despite my own continuing loyalty for many reasons to my Protestant heritage, I do not look for the creative reinterpretation of Christianity to appear in the next decade from Protestantism.[11]

We turn then to Catholicism as the possible source or matrix for a creative modern Christianity. In outlining the reasons why I think such a synthesis may well arise there, if it is to arise at all, I shall point to elements of present Catholic life that seem to me not only to manifest genuine aspects of the biblical view of the people of God, but also to provide the most hopeful prospects for the immediate Christian future. These elements are signs of great potential strength in Catholic life and thus immensely relevant to both present and future needs. In enumerating these elements of strength I am *not* seeking to "define" Catholicism or authentic Catholicism. Such is not and could not be my task. There is, for example, no discussion of the apostolic succession, or of the role in that succession of the bishop of Rome, "marks" of the church that would of necessity be central to any serious definition or theological understanding of Catholicism or Roman Catholicism. In fact it is just such a discussion among Catholics of the "essential nature" of Catholicism *in the modern setting* that I am calling for if there is to be new life. To be relevant, such a discussion must be both open and experimental, and at the same time concerned with these and other basic "marks" of the church. It must be willing to risk being called "heretical" about Catholic fundamentals if it is to be of any use. But this is not my purpose here. My point is merely to say what is biblical and promising of new life in the present Catholic church, however she be defined.

When I ask myself why I expect this new life in Catholicism, with its confusion, discord, disarray, and potential disintegration, there are several answers. First of all there is the *catholic* (universal) character of the Roman church, representing far more than do Protestantism, Anglicanism, or Orthodoxy, all classes, nations, continents, and races. No one Christian communion spans so many cultures or brings together so much of the human family into one people. To be sure, the World Council does; but no more than the assembled bishops, is the World Council a people! Even more important than this catholicity or scope, however, is the Catholic sense of a concrete or substantive *people*, an actual social community among the other communities of history with both visible and invisible bonds. This community is a substantive historical *entity* over and above the individuals in it, continuous over time, and present in our social world so that every member participates in that real community as a Christian. Clearly this Catholic sense of a unique, substantive, historical community extending over time and space derives from the traditional belief that the church represents the mystical Body of Christ,[12] a divine-human institution, blessed and invigorated by the divine spirit and by its head, Christ. It is an earthly society, but one constituted, set apart, and ruled by its transcendent head rather than merely by the human individuals who make it up. It is, therefore, a society with supernatural reality, identity, authority, powers, and grace. Whether the sense of being a unique *people* can remain amid the present shattering of the church's traditional supernaturalistic forms of authority, rule, and unity is problematical. In America and other religiously pluralistic societies with upward mobility out of specific Catholic "ghettoes," its survival is called in question. Whether this Catholic sense can withstand the loss of common traditional habits of life, belief, and worship remains to be seen. But the Catholic sense of a *historical people* is authentically biblical, and perhaps the most precious inheritance of Catholic life in the present. It can, if it survives, provide the indispensable communal matrix for creative new forms.

If one asks what characterizes the identity of this people, besides the traits of traditional beliefs, thought, life, and worship that were once its visible "marks," four things come to mind. These characteristics are peculiarly Catholic and have great contemporary power and relevance.

1. There is a sense of the reality, importance, and "weight" of tradition and history in the formation of this people and so of her religious truths, religious experience, and human wisdom. To be sure, such a devotion to tradition, if given an absolute and supernatural authority and weight, can be stifling and corrupt, when merely external and so potentially hypocritical. Nevertheless, in a secular age with little sense of or need for historical roots, and in a religion itself based on history but increasingly aware only of the present and the future, such an awareness and appreciation of tradition can be a source of vast strength. The burning question is: can tradition still be valued when its supernatural authority has been qualified by the relativism of modernity?

2. There is, especially to a Protestant, a remarkable sense of humanity and grace in the communal life of Catholics. Compared to Protestants, Catholics seem to be far less "uptight" about the moral rules their grandfathers held. There is a deeper recognition of the final inability of good and bad alike to adhere to these rules, and so a more Christian tolerance and acceptance of the estranged and

fallible characteristics of our lives. Strangely, considering
the origins in history of the two communities, Catholics
are presently "free of the law" in comparison with Protestants. Consequently the love of life, the appreciation of
the body and the senses, of joy and celebration, the tolerance of the sinner, these natural, worldly and "human"
virtues are far more clearly and universally embodied in
Catholics and in Catholic life than in Protestants and in
Protestantism. Perhaps in the mystery of God's providence the traditional rules and practices of Catholic life
on moral, especially sexual, matters were *so* fantastic, *so*
irrelevant and stifling, *so* inconceivably "uptight," in effect
*so* heteronomous and objective, that (except for the "religious") they never encased or bound the inner Catholic
soul (though they determined it from the outside in terms
of behavior) in the same way that the far more sensible,
moral, and above all, more inward Protestant ethic on
such matters surely encased and so bound the Protestant
soul.

Thus while the official and objective structures of Catholicism still reflect an anti-natural, anti-sensual, moralistic, and even ascetic view of general human existence
and its goods, Catholic life itself—for the laity and now
for much of the clergy—reflects a freedom from moralistic
prohibitions and judgments of other people that is the
envy of many Protestants. Again the roots of this tolerance in moral affairs amid deep commitment, this charity
of spirit, lie, first, in the traditional Catholic distinction
between two levels of value, and so two levels of Christian
life, one natural and the other supernatural; and, second,
in the objectivity of sacred law and of holiness in Catholicism generally.[13] Can this love of life combined with
Christian concern and charity remain? Will it continue
when the distinction disappears between those two levels
and the objectivity of divine law is questioned? These are

among the most important questions for contemporary Catholicism.

In an age fortunately moving away from the moralism of the past two or three centuries, there seems to be the basis in Catholic lay and present clerical life for a new understanding of personal Christian existence, less moralistic and legalistic, more sensual and celebratory, more charitable and tolerant. Furthermore, these characteristics of Catholicism already mentioned—the sense of the substantive *people* in history, separable if not separate from the nations, and the sense of the *tradition* of that people under God—have combined with a new commitment and concern for the world and for men and women in the world to bring forth ethical fruits of vast social and historical relevance. For in our time a visible Catholic protest against what is evil and destructive in present human society has assumed major proportions; and a sizable movement in that church for justice and liberation in the world may well appear.[14] Within this tradition there seems to be possible a greater sense of critical distance from society, and so a reformist and even a radical stance toward it, than in a more "worldly" Protestantism. Once, therefore, the supernatural and the ecclesiastical interpretations of traditional Catholic *caritas* or concern recede, and the church ceases to look only upward and inward; and once the concentration of this undoubtedly potent force turns outward to issues of justice in our present communal life, Catholics may well actively enter the world and yet, in a strange way retaining distance from it, be vastly creative for its future. Thus the social gospel and the political theologies developed first in recent Protestant circles, but immobilized in the bourgeois setting of Protestantism, may find in the decades to come more creative embodiment in Catholicism than anywhere else. With Catholicism lies the possibility of a creative application of

the New Testament sense of tolerance, charity, and concern for the world's life to modern social injustices and
miseries.

3. Next, Catholicism has had a continuing experience, unequalled in other forms of Western Christianity,
of the presence of God and of grace mediated through
symbols to the entire course of ordinary human life. Three
elements of this continuing experience of grace are important in this connection: the sense of transcendent mystery
impinging continually on human existence as its source
and ground and as the principle of its healing and hope;
the communication of this experience through a wide
variety or range of symbols—material, sensuous, aesthetic, active, verbal, and intellectual; and the sense of the
utter importance of this "sacramental" communication of
grace for each stage and each crisis of ordinary human
beings in the world. Manifestly, this Catholic experience
of grace has been embodied within ancient, even archaic,
liturgical structures often almost magical in character,
and within rites and practices often openly superstitious
in their forms. That experience has depended historically
on the deep belief that the mystical Body of Christ that
mediated grace through these structures, sacraments,
rites, and obligations possessed an objective supernatural
grace and an absolute authority over dogma and law. As
the process of liberal reform progressively dissolves the
more archaic forms of these liturgical and sacramental
structures, and weakens the supernatural and absolute
authority of the institution that mediates them, possibly
this central sacramental sense of the holy will also be
shaken and even threatened. The heart of the conservative
argument is that the traditional forms of Catholic liturgy,
practice, and dogma, and the church's absolute supernatural authority, are essential to her mediatorial role,
and to the communication of sacramental grace to mankind. For this view reform on either account has been and

will increasingly be fatal to her mission and even her life.[15]

The validity of this argument is possibly the deepest issue of the current debate. But it might not be irrelevant for an observer to advance the odd thesis that this "sacramental" form of religion, communicating grace through a variety of symbols to the entire span of ordinary life, may have a special relevance to modern needs and problems. Our contemporary spirit possesses an apprehension of the deepest relativity and change, and so of the relativity of our concepts and our speech on the one hand and of our inner feelings on the other. This sense of the relativity of both concepts and feelings is accompanied by a new awareness of the equal value of the sensual and the bodily to that of the verbal and the intellectual. In such a situation this sacramental emphasis on symbol may well have more creative possibilities than a concentration on the proclaimed Word. For symbols can be sensuous, aesthetic, and celebratory as well as verbal and intellectual. And in a relativistic age they can probably communicate more authentically and define less literally the divine mystery, glory, and promise. On the other hand, the sacramental concern for the continuous relevance of grace to all the structures of ordinary, natural life can possibly relate the holy to our common individual and our common social life more effectively than can a piety based solely on proclamation from the pulpit. It is strange but understandable that a sacramental and so symbolic mode of religiosity may possess more creative possibilities within modernity than either the classical Protestant emphasis on the sacred Word alone or the spiritualistic Protestant (and now pentecostal) emphasis on a transrational presence of the Spirit. For a symbol combines, without destroying either one, absoluteness and relativity better than either propositional dogmas or verbal proclamation. The symbol points to and communicates a divinity that lies beyond it;

it can be viewed and appropriated as *relative*, as a "symbol" and not God, without sacrificing this relation to the *absoluteness* that makes it a vehicle of the sacred. This is more difficult for verbal and intellectual media—stated dogmas, doctrines, or preaching—that are either absolute and authoritative or human and relative, and rarely appropriated as both.

Furthermore, the experience of the symbol can unite sensual, aesthetic, and intellectual experience more readily than the experiences of proclamation or of an ecstatic spiritual presence. Quite possibly, therefore, the "Catholic principle" that communicates the divine mystery, not merely through rational consciousness nor through ecstasy alone, but through a wide range of symbols related to all the facets of ordinary life, may in the end turn out to be the least anachronistic, "superstitious," and restrictive of all. In fact it may provide the best entrance into a new synthesis of the Christian tradition with the vitalities as well as the relativities of contemporary existence. Thus the possibility of a valid and authentic form of Christianity for our time depends largely on the creative ability of contemporary Catholicism to separate the sacramental principle from the objectivist, absolutist, and anachronistic embodiments in which it was imprisoned and recently made ineffective, and to reinterpret and re-embody that principle in *contemporary* terms. What such a restructuring of these four essential traits of Catholicism—people, tradition, *caritas*, and sacramental presence—might look like, only a Catholic can or should say. But a sympathetic observer may well state that *this* is where the hope of a revitalized Christianity probably lies.

4. Finally, there has been throughout Catholic history a drive toward rationality, the insistence that the divine mystery manifest in tradition and sacramental presence be insofar as is possible penetrated, defended, and explicated by the most acute rational reflection. The value of

this traditional insistence in an age concerned with cognitive certainty and reflective clarity is undoubted, and is one of the main reasons that Catholicism has such an important role to play in the Christian future. And yet traditionally this drive toward rationality has, to an outsider, combined in a most strange way the unquestioned and even unquestionable authority of tradition with a similarly uncriticized philosophy. One might say that in traditional Catholic life the speculative but not the critical powers of reason were accepted. Thus Catholicism ran directly counter to the main themes of the later Enlightenment and modern empiricism, which have stressed these critical powers as a necessary if not a sufficient condition of any relation to the truth. Part of the intellectual crisis of the present lies here: once critical reason was accepted on the part of many Catholics, the whole rational edifice of the tradition collapsed into what was now to them *un*-reason. The crucial question before the church now on this issue is whether this persistent rationality can successfully express itself within the context of a new view of the authority of revelation and a new understanding of the relation of critical philosophy to theological affirmation.

In each case the present change, confusion, and disarray in the traditional and supernatural structures of Catholicism appear unquestionably to threaten her central attributes and sources of strength: the unity and substantiality of the *people* as community, the reality of *tradition*, the grace of *caritas* in her life and mission, the *sacramental* sense of the living presence of God—of the transcendent and the holy mystery of God—through concrete, material, aesthetic, verbal, and intellectual symbols, and the *rationality* of the traditional faith. How deep that threat to this essence may be, there is no telling. One can only repeat the faith that the church will endure, and endure creatively amidst even the most inescapable and shattering of changes. But, interestingly, this same change and confusion has revealed as much as threatened these elements of creativity latent within Catholicism. For each of these creative principles found its historical embodiment within traditional forms now rendered problematic by modernity. These traditional supernaturalistic forms not only expressed and sustained creative "Catholic" elements but also in the modern period the old forms became more and more stifling, threatening to kill the potential creativity of Catholicism.

The *people* as an historical social and ecclesiastical entity was defined and maintained, theologically and institutionally, by a forced unity of doctrine, law, and common practice, and this unity was achieved through an absolute obedience to an infallible authority above error and historical change. It was defined and maintained sociologically by the trivial, and increasingly anachronistic, habits of ecclesiastical and often local history, in this case "ghetto" history. These forces unifying Catholicism into one people, one force ecclesiastical and the other sociological, stifled both creativity and relevance. For Catholic life—intellectually, morally, and sociologically—was on the whole frozen into the changeless compartments of traditional ways, set apart at each level from the life of modernity, and thus more and more empty of authenticity and valid inner content. Only when the diverse and relativizing forces of modern life had begun to dissolve these traditional forms of authority and unity and to break down the walls of the Catholic ghettos, could the creative vitality of the *people* in Catholic life be seen. Only then could a new synthesis be conceived. And only when the absolute authority of an heteronomous and ascetic moral law was qualified could the creative humanity and grace in Catholic life take on its true grandeur.

*Tradition* as the living ground of present life was embodied in absolute forms of dogma, doctrine, law, and liturgical practice. To repeat these forms was to be "in" tradition, and to change or to vary them was to depart from tradition. Each specific traditional form, no matter how particular its origin in time or place, held all the absolute status and sanction of the supernatural origin of the whole tradition itself. Thus Tradition, a historical category, was de-historicized, *aufgehoben* into supernature, eternity, and absoluteness; and the creativity of a living tradition—a necessary corollary to its traditional character—was sacrificed and almost lost.[16] Again, the historical consciousness of modernity (that all that is in time partakes of historical relativity) and the existential, personal, or autonomous consciousness of modernity (that what is meaningful to me must be said in *my* terms) have dissolved these absolute forms of tradition, and thus freed tradition to be itself. This freedom allows tradition to communicate the presence of God in and through past events, a communication borne, interpreted and reinterpreted by the community that in its history witnesses to those events.[17] For a *historical* people is in essence traditional, created out of and by history and constituted in each age by its continuity with its past. Once, therefore, man has come to understand himself *historically*, as modernity has surely come to understand him, the Catholic emphasis on tradition as the source and ground of the present could become (once that tradition in turn ceased to be absolute because "supernatural") extremely relevant to the modern situation. But again it took these convulsions introduced by modernity to show this.

The relevance and creativity of the *sacramental* principle were also obscured by the traditional, absolute forms in which they were embodied. For the symbols that mediated the divine mystery were themselves divinized, or at least made changeless, errorless, and self-sufficient as vehicles of divine truth and grace. One hardly needed to penetrate through them to the divine mystery itself or outside of them to other symbolic accounts; they were *a se*, the ground of truth and grace rather than their relative media. Thus these absolute dogmatic and sacramental symbols hid rather than mediated the living mystery and presence of God. In the eyes of many Catholic commentators, they eventually replaced that mystery and that presence: the sense of mystery eroded in the precision of absolute dogmatic statements; the presence of the mystery of grace faded in the mere repetition of sacred formulas and sacred actions; and the necessity of that mystery to our human existence was unapprehended in the extrinsic mode in which such "supernatural" symbols inevitably related to the autonomous human consciousness. Again, the modern sense of the relativity of all symbolic forms, and the necessity of personal appropriation if they are to be authentic symbols, freed the mystery behind them to communicate itself through them to us in our space and time. The way was thus opened for a new understanding of the divine presence that supports, illumines, and heals rather than denies the modern sense of universal relativity, and that encourages rather than ignores the modern emphasis on personal appropriation of all that is humanly significant.

The persistent and impressive rationality of Catholicism was based on a synthesis of reason and faith that has now become outmoded. This synthesis was in turn dependent upon a division of labor between a speculative philosophy that dealt with the experienced realm of nature, and a sacred doctrine founded on a definitive revelation of truths coming from and concerning a transnatural and transrational divine realm. Thus could the philosophy remain autonomous and the theology be protected from the threats of critical philosophy. Because of this ancient division there is still—to the surprise of a visitor to Catholic faculties—a distinct separation between a Catholic philosophical faculty and a Catholic theological faculty, between clerical philosophers and clerical theologians, as if what each talked about had little or nothing to do with the concerns of the other!

Now my point is that in the modern situation I do not consider either useful or rational this traditionally sharp division between philosophy concerned only with natural experience—and so not with theology—and a sacred theology concerned only with propositions and dogmas of revelation—and so not with philosophical criticism. If this is correct, the division and synthesis based on it must be revised in order for the rationality of Catholicism to be creative in the present and in the future, as surely it can and must be. An illustration of this new interrelation between the realm appropriate to philosophy and that appropriate to theology is the fact that most of the themes in modernity that have challenged traditional Catholic *theological* foundations, and raised the *ecclesiastical* issues I have pointed to, are philosophical themes, or more appropriately, ways of viewing man and his world that have been most potently expressed in modern philosophies. More formally, the entire relation between philosophy and theology has been transformed in the intervening period since this division between the two was first formulated centuries ago. Inevitably, in the present the two overlap and interpenetrate, and thus they cannot be neatly separated into natural and supernatural compartments as once was the case.

There are two reasons for this fundamental change in the relation of philosophical reason to faith and the transformed relation of the two disciplines to each other. The first is that the division between nature and supernature, the one realm appropriate for an autonomous philosophy and the other for an autonomous theology, is no longer tenable in the older form. In some strange way we live now in one world, the pervasive structures of which are appropriate for philosophical inquiry and the depth of which is appropriate for theology, but no *clear* line of division is possible between them. Consequently the two are interdependent in ways not characteristic of the traditional division. If philosophy is now considered quite autonomous and given unlimited range, there is then, as most modern philosophy shows, no room for theology at all, since a realm quite beyond the natural is no longer "there" for us. This is a point that Catholics enthusiastic for unlimited philosophical rationality might take to heart. If, on the other hand, theology is now considered autonomous within this one world, there is no room for a philosophy relevant to theology, and barely any role for philosophy at all, as Protestant neo-orthodoxy indicates. If both are to be there, they will have to be seen as inter-penetrating in new ways. Thus Catholic theologians are driven also to be philosophers. In turn *Catholic* philosophers may have to find the roots of their philosophy in the religious depths of experience and thus at the most fundamental level join with Catholic theology, as Karl Rahner so beautifully illustrates. Faith and reason do not deal with different realms. Rather, they are different aspects of every passive, cognitive, and active encounter with reality. Catholic philosophy and theology in this new world must not remain merely side by side, or one on top of the other, lest so isolated each wither and die.

The second reason for the new relation between Catholic reason and Catholic faith is that divine revelation does not come to us anymore in unambiguously sacred and authoritative propositions that are therefore autonomous or independent of experiential grounding and ultimately independent of philosophical questioning. We cannot merely deduce our theologies by historical inquiry and speculative thought from given sacred data since, as Bernard Lonergan has noted, such sacred data simply do not exist. Theology, therefore, if it is to find a ground for its own authority and its own content, is of necessity much more intimately related to experience than it once was, and so to philosophical criticism and thematization of that experience. Just as a Catholic philosopher must now recognize the religious and theological roots of his philosophy, if it is to make room for the theology he also espouses, so a Catholic theologian must—and this has already happened—recognize the dependence of his theological ideas on contemporary philosophical themes and explications.

Finally, because of the supernatural and absolute character of her doctrines, the intellectual life of this wide community—rich in learning, intelligence, and devotion —was more archaic, trivial, and defensive than it might otherwise have been.[18] Too many intelligent Catholic minds approached other points of view only to counter them; for to them the entire truth was already possessed. Too much logical thought was spent offering ever more fantastic arguments for traditional formulations increasingly out of date and incredible. And whenever novel interpretations did appear, too much scholarly energy was spent endlessly combing an authoritative tradition for vindication of this new insight. Only in those areas where the weight of supernatural, absolute authority did not rest so heavily, did creative Catholic intellect really manifest itself: in philosophy and in historical studies, although again neither was as free or rich and creative as it might have been. Thus once again when modernity had dissolved this absolute, supernatural authority over the present mind (which in effect meant the authority of thirteenth- or seventeenth-century minds over twentieth-century ones!) the Catholic theological mind was free to show its vast intellectual creativity as well as its monumental learning. And it now easily dominates, as it has not since the fifteenth century, the Christian theological scene. As this history amply illustrates, the shaking of established structures in history is threatening and possibly even mortal; but it is also the necessary condition for creative historical change and contemporary relevance. Paradoxically, therefore, only out of the institutional and intellectual chaos such as present Catholicism is experiencing, could an authentic revival of *Catholicism* occur, and an authentic *Catholic* synthesis of modernity and the gospel be achieved. For her archaic, absolute structures had obscured in our age her own creative potentiality as *Catholic*, and thus much of the meaning for us all of our common gospel, since it reduced the power of the modern Catholic minds seeking for that meaning.

If the possibility of creativity arises *because* the old is being shaken and not despite that fact, then it is clear that the present confusion of authority, doctrines, law, customs, and usages of Catholic life must be accepted, faced, and understood in all its radical depth, and then interpreted *positively*, to make that creativity possible. It is not enough to say that Catholics are and always have been "a people"; that they have and always have had a sense of tradition; that they have and always have had a sense of *caritas*, tolerance, and concern for one another; that they understand and live from the sacraments and always have done so. Merely agreeing that this is now so, and always has been, will not make possible the appropriation of the potential creativity in each of these elements of Catholic life. For each principle has been enshrined in forms that in the end *obscured* that creativity; and thus each must be transformed and reinterpreted radically, if a new and relevant form of Catholicism—a Christianity that expresses these four principles—is to be possible. To find what is permanent, essential, and validly traditional in Catholic life we must penetrate through, refashion, and even possibly discard precisely what has *appeared* to be permanent, essential, and traditional in Catholicism; in order to reach *authentic tradition* we must in truth *begin anew*. This effort is admittedly paradoxical, but it is nonetheless true. For what had appeared permanent has historically dissolved; and before it dissolved it stifled what was essentially there. And above all, an authentic people, tradition, *caritas*, and sacramental presence will arise in modernity only in the forms of consciousness, community, truth, and personal being characteristic of modernity. Thus the confusion and disintegration of the present, its social, theological, and religious chaos, must be accepted and understood as the positive precondition for new relevant and creative life. No Protestant can envision this Catholic synthesis or even substantially contribute to it. But possibly a Protestant can help Catholics to understand what has happened and what is happening to them. For the Protestant has been through much of this himself over a longer period of time, and he may understand better the nature of the storm because of that long experience.

The most fundamental issues for any form of Christianity—or for any form of religion, for that matter—lie of course in those perennial structures of the human condition that resist man's obedience to God and so his own fulfillment, structures symbolized classically by fate, sin, and death. The primary forms of crisis for religion always arise from human recalcitrance and pride; and the consequent effort on the part of us all to deal with fate and death on human rather than divine terms. Fate, sin, and death have been *there* in every age, probably in equal amount, though awareness of their reality and power apparently varies from epoch to epoch. It is to them that the gospel perennially addresses itself; to deal with them divine grace has been given to men; and to cope as best as it can with them the church, the people of God, is present in history. In this sense the deepest problems facing any form of Christianity are constant, invariant in relation to that form's cultural and historical situation. Conservatives are right insofar as they emphasize these changeless

problems of sin, fate, and death, the utter inability of anything except the transcendent to cope with them, and so
the changeless gift and promise of divine grace to the
church as the sole essential basis of its health, authenticity, creative power, and authority.

Despite these constant factors in the history of the
church, there are also other, perhaps secondary, factors
variable with its cultural situation that vitally affect the
authenticity and integrity of the church's life, and thus its
ability to embody and mediate divine grace. These effects
of culture on religion and the church are immense;
scarcely any form of piety, theology, ethic or liturgical
usage, any conception of the church's mission and tasks,
or any institutional structure of clerical or lay life, fails to
be molded by the ideas, attitudes, values, and forms that
prevail in the society in which that religion lives. Forms
of religious and ecclesiastical life, therefore, reflect the
forms of cultural existence in which they appear, and in
that sense every form of religion is dependent upon, an
expression of, its culture. On the other hand, cultural life
itself manifests in its own way the crises of fate, sin, and
death, and thus in its turn requires the presence of religion and of healing grace to life in history that religion
mediates. This dependence of church life on its culture
means that what we may call a *secondary level* of crisis
can arise within the church as a result of the interacting
of the church with the forms of culture within which it
lives. For the purposes of our discussion, such "secondary"
crises in turn subsist on two levels,[19] arising from two
different sources within social life.

First of all, cultures, the forms of social existence, are
"historical" and thus continually subject to change: ways
of seeing the self, others, and the world can change radically as they have done continuously in history. Thus
forms of religion developed in another cultural epoch and
enshrining their religious ideas, norms, and roles in the

shapes of that past cultural existence can become, when historical changes occur, anachronistic, oppressive, even possibly demonic, and certainly irrelevant in the new age. Liberals are rightly aware of this fact of historical change and its effect on the relevance and power of all the older forms of a religion's life, and this awareness justifies their efforts in every period when cultural change has occurred to reform or modernize the church, to "bring the church up to date," and thus to make it more relevant, meaningful, and effective in contemporary existence.

Second, certain cultural epochs are more "religious" in the tone and form of their life than are others; correspondingly, certain epochs are more "secular." This is *not* to say that the primary issues with which Christian faith must deal—fate, sin, and death—are *less* in a religious culture and *more* in a secular one, for that is clearly not the case. And, manifestly, much that is creative both in life and in religion arises out of a "secular" form of cultural life—as is clearly the case with the Enlightenment. In fact a good case could be made that the secularity of modern culture has *some* of its roots in the biblical tradition. Still, in a secular culture, religion and thus Christianity, and with them the reality of God and thus the deeper categories of divine grace, revelation, and responding faith, are themselves subjected to critical attack as unreal, irrelevant, and outmoded. In such a case it is not primarily the *ancient* character of religion that is criticized, as it is by the liberal believer; rather, it is religion *itself* as a relation to any transcendent reality, religion in old *or* modern dress, that is under criticism by many of the most potent and influential of the spiritual and intellectual forces of the culture. The dominant or "establishment" side of the culture of our own age is of this sort. Now whether such an age is as secular in its existence as it believes, or as it seeks to be in its explicit thought patterns, is another question.

There seems to be little doubt, however, that such a cultural mood adds a new and serious level of problems for those who would wish either to commend or to proclaim the Christian faith to themselves or to others. As has been widely witnessed among people inside and outside the churches, there is in such an age an experience of the absence of God, or even a total absence of the experience of God. Correspondingly, there is either an unwarranted confidence in the self-sufficiency of human capacities and institutions to deal with the problems of life, or a crippling sense of despair over their resolution in any form. And, as a final consequence, there is a widespread feeling of the irrelevance and futility of religious faith and commitment, and a sense of the meaninglessness and lack of validity of religious language. In such a situation many lose their interest in religion (whether in traditional or modern, conservative or liberal form), their concern for revelation (whether in orthodox or in neo-orthodox form), their sense of dependence on grace and the divine promises, however any of these are understood, proclaimed, or liturgically embodied. Such persons may leave the church or remain within it; in the latter case, since the *religious* dimensions of its life—and the categories of sin, revelation, and grace—have ceased to have meaning or validity for them, it is to other aspects of the church's life, i.e., solely to her works of ministry or the healing aspects of her human community, that they give their attention and interest.[20]

Perhaps the main thesis of this book is that modernity, as the culture within which the clergy and the laity in the Catholic church now largely live, has faced Roman Catholicism at the same instant with precisely this double set of problems or crises, and that the two levels or aspects of the crisis of modernity interact on each other, making the situation more confusing and more bitter. Further, unlike Catholicism, Protestantism has in one way

or another, both successfully and unsuccessfully, sought
for two hundred years or more to deal with, absorb, and
reinterpret the culture of modernity—a modernity that
has developed more and more radically over those two
centuries. Thus Protestantism has had the good fortune to
be able to see the structure and the effects of this interaction of Christianity and modernity slowly unfold before it,
first on one level and then on the other. Catholicism, on
the other hand, has really for the first time tried to absorb
the effects of this whole vast modern development from
the Enlightenment to the present in the short period between 1963 and 1973! Thus *all* the spiritual, social, and
technological forces that have structured and transformed
the modern history of the West have suddenly, and without much preparation, impinged forcefully on her life,
and they have had to be comprehended, reinterpreted,
and dealt with by Catholicism in one frantic decade.
There has been little time in which to understand what
these forces are, or what it is they do or threaten to do to
Christianity or to traditional Catholicism; it has been impossible to discriminate these various levels of the problem as it developed. No wonder the picture is one of intense confusion and chaos: the structure or anatomy of
the interaction between Catholic Christianity and modernity, and the meaning of the various responses of the
church to that interaction, have been almost hopelessly
blurred. Let us see now if we can by analysis expose the
anatomy of that interaction. With regard to modernity,
Protestantism is "the elder brother"; perhaps a Protestant,
long used to pondering the interaction of modernity with
his own tradition, can help illuminate this interaction,
even if he cannot possibly assist in the reinterpretation of
Catholicism that must result from such understanding.

The first aspect or level of the crisis induced by modernity, familiar to us all, results from the pervasive aspect of
*change* in cultural and historical life. Roman Catholicism

was shaped essentially as a form of religious life through its patristic and definitively through its medieval inheritance. These forms, enshrined in its creeds and dogmas, theological and philosophical elaborations, canon laws, sacramental and liturgical practices, and ecclesiastical structures, remained remarkably unchanged from those ages to this—interpreted, debated, sharpened, reformulated, increasingly objectified and rationalized, to be sure, but surprisingly the same from the fourth and fifth through the thirteenth to the twentieth centuries. However, the culture in which this edifice existed has subsequently undergone vast changes: in fundamental structures of beliefs, in views of what is real, true, and of value in the world and in mankind, in social institutions and practices, in modes and styles of life. Much of this modern world (approximately the eighteenth-century Enlightenment to the present) had clearly seeped into Catholic attitudes and life, especially among its educated elite. But much had also been kept out, and what elements of modernity were there were (as the modernist and pre-Vatican II "liberalizers" manifested to others and discovered for themselves) rigidly controlled and confined, restricted to certain areas of thought and life but taboo in other areas—in fact taboo in all *fundamental* areas.

When in Vatican II, by the strange processes and inevitabilities of history, these restrictions were lifted and the church sought deliberately to adjust herself to this new and different world, by reinterpretating the forms of her thought and life in some yet unspecified measure in modern terms, the *first* level of the problem appeared on the scene: how does a religion that seeks to preserve its identity deal with historical change? Or, more precisely, how are the *old* forms to be given a *new* shape in tune with the modernity we live in? Given a modernity in thought, norms, and usages, to which the church seeks to adjust her faith and her life, what is the relation of such a modernity to these traditional structures of dogma, theology, philosophy, law, authority, sacrament, and custom in which the faith is enshrined but which "we" (or some of us) wish to "update"? Does the updating of our traditional inheritance merely entail changes on the surface of these traditional structures—as when a nun is allowed to wear a new costume or to drive a car, or a priest to read Protestant or secular books? Or is this new relation to modernity to result in fundamental reinterpretations of these patristic and medieval structures, setting them in new forms radically different from those of traditional Catholic usage, but preserving, if possible, their Catholic substance and essentially their basic Christian character? For the first or "conservative" interpretation of *aggiornamento*, authentic Catholicism *meant* those older, traditional structures, and so change was to be admitted only cautiously in order not to involve them.[21] Consequently, no fundamental *aggiornamento* was to be permitted in basic dogmas, theology, canon law, mission, or ecclesiastical structure. For the second, the "liberal" interpretation of *aggiornamento*, the older structures were now empty and powerless, lacking in spiritual authority and moral relevance, and thus they were impediments to, rather than the vehicles of, either grace or authentic Catholicism. Consequently for these liberals a reinterpretation of Catholicism in modern terms was necessary across the board: dogmas, theology, authority, ethics, mission in the world, and liturgy alike were to be reconceived in the light of modern attitudes, norms, goals, and philosophies. And (so they argued) as the original gospel had been thoroughly reconceived in Hellenistic and then in feudal terms, so in the present day a thoroughly new reconception is necessary. Thus arose most of the explicit arguments of the council and of the post-*aggiornamento* age: between those who wished to allow no, or at most a minimal, reinterpretation of dogma and those who did;

between the defenders of neo-Thomist theology and philosophy and the champions of modern forms of each; between those who saw the church's mission in supernatural terms and those who saw it in historical and even political terms; between those defending the older forms of liturgy and those espousing the vernacular and new forms; and so on through issues of ecclesiastical authority, theological education and formation, family and sexual ethics, to celibacy and social radicalism.

These issues were drawn between older forms of *religion* and new, modern forms of *religion*. The question was, not whether religion was possible in modernity, but whether a viable modern Catholicism should at its most fundamental levels be set in traditional or in modern forms; and if either, how much of the other was necessary, permissible, and safe. To the conservatives, only that minimal amount of modernization was permissible that would keep Catholicism in touch with the world, but not to transform it fundamentally. Wherever the "sacred heart" of Catholicism was reached, modernization—and even discussion—must perforce cease, for then Catholicism itself was in danger, a Catholicism that was assumed to be identical with these endangered forms. To the liberals, on the contrary, enough traditional elements should be preserved to retain Catholicism's essential touch with its past character and so with its historical identity. But because the forms within which that identity had been traditionally embodied were relative to their time, and so in a new age obscured rather than mediated grace, across-the-board reinterpretation was necessary for that Catholic identity to come alive as a *religious* force in our age as it had in the creative periods of the past.

Since religions exist within a continuum of historical change, such arguments between traditionalists and modernists, conservatives and liberals, are only to be expected, once the issue of *aggiornamento* is frankly raised. They were characteristic of both the patristic and medieval periods, and they have manifestly dominated Protestant life since the Enlightenment with regard to *its* fundamental and essential structures: scriptural authority and confessional theology in relation to modern philosophy and science; personal and social ethics in relation to modern concepts of individual and social good; the authority, role, and style of the clergy, and so on. These are crucial matters of debate for any form of the church and must be carried on responsibly and seriously. The most obvious requirement for such a responsible debate is that open discussion be carried on concerning the nature of the historical changes that surround us, their effects on all levels of Catholic faith and life, and, most importantly, the most essential elements of *Catholic* Christianity that in a world of change must be preserved and encouraged. For the theological community to refuse to debate frankly and freely the *fundamentals* of Christian and Catholic life—and thus to refuse the "risk" of being considered by some to be "un-Catholic"—is for the church to beg entirely the question with which the reality of historical change inescapably faces us all.

I would suggest, however, that in both the Protestant and the present Catholic cases these conflicts between conservatives and liberals have been vastly deepened and confused by the presence of the *second* level of the crisis, and that much of the sense of ultimacy involved in the conflicts, and so their bitterness, have been caused by the anxieties and fears generated out of this second level. By the second level I refer to the quite different issue of whether *any* religious existence, thought, or goals in the world are viable in the modern age, be they ancient or modern, traditional or liberal, socially conservative or radical in form.

My point is that had the modern age not been so radically "secularistic" in its self-understanding, *aggiorna-*

*mento* would not have had the seemingly bitter and destructive results that have dismayed almost everyone on
both sides of the issue. For then modern forms of religiosity and faith would have had the same intrinsic relation to
the Catholic substance as traditional ones. As the liberals
had hoped at Vatican II, bringing the church "up to date"
would only have strengthened and revitalized the church
and made her a stronger rather than a weaker force
among her people and in the world. But the modern age *is*
secular, and modern forms of thought and life fit uneasily,
if at all, into *any* Christian framework. *Aggiornamento*
potentially can mean, therefore, not only bringing this
church up to date by giving her modern form; it can also
mean bringing her fully into a secularistic world in which
she can barely survive, in which not only her traditional
forms but also her faith at the most fundamental levels are
shaken. In fact both have happened, and at the same moment, so that the two crises, or the two levels of the same
crisis, are difficult to distinguish. When the process of *aggiornamento* "opened the windows of the church" to the
fresh breezes of modernity, those open windows also let in
the chill blasts of naturalistic atheism and indifference, of
a form of secularistic thought and life antithetical to religion of any sort and so to any interpretation of the Christian faith, ancient or modern. Because of this latter, more
chilling aspect of modernity, conservatives, who felt
deeply this danger, were ultimately afraid of all fundamental liberal reformulations—not only that they would
weaken Catholicism's traditional forms, but that in so
doing they would destroy Catholicism itself. For as many
explicitly stated and many more undoubtedly implicitly
felt, the forms of a secular age are essentially antithetical
to Catholicism in a way that those of former religious ages
were not. The pre-Vatican II neoscholastic (and elitist)
nostalgia for the "religious age" of the thirteenth century
became after Vatican II the visceral basis of curial and

conservative reaction to all attempts to modernize. Each expressed the deep, by no means irrational, fear that modernity was identical to secularistic atheism and humanism and thus fatal to the very being of the church. Correspondingly, liberals were by the same awareness driven to despise the traditionalist as a danger to Catholicism. Not only did liberals feel that archaic forms were now uncreative and irrelevant to them personally as "modern men." Even more they were convinced—and also on very plausible grounds—that a Christianity embodied in such archaic and extrinsic forms had no possibility at all of stemming the tide of secular indifference and atheism, or of preventing the final eradication of faith itself. On both sides the quite understandable fear that the opponent, unconsciously to be sure, was aiding and abetting the forces of secular atheism in our time confused and so embittered the issues debated by conservatives and liberals as *aggiornamento* proceeded.

Perhaps the most important way that the reality and power of these secular forces have deepened that crisis is in the "existential" area. For the possibility of a viable personal existence—at least on the surface of life—unrelated to church or religion is a new and very real option that modernity offers. This offer of a "religionless life" is the "existential" side of modernity's secularism as its naturalistic and positivistic viewpoints and philosophies form its "reflective" side. The possibility for a secular *existence* appeared for the first time to countless Catholics—for whom previously a secularistic self-understanding had been literally inconceivable—the moment *aggiornamento* began. This possibility of a *non*-Catholic identity is quite distinct from the possibility of a liberal or reformed Catholic identity. Both appeared with *aggiornamento*, and so at one and the same time; but they ought not to be confused with one another, for they represent totally different stances vis-à-vis Catholicism and modernity. This new secular possibility challenged both the relevance of newer, more liberal forms of Catholicism as they appeared and the continuing value of the now weakened older structures. Thus when those conservatives dismayed by new changes in the church, others discouraged by conflicts there, or those liberals frustrated by the slowness of reform, came for the first time to discover through *aggiornamento* the possibility of a secular, nonreligious, non-Christian existence, they were frequently driven to abandon the church entirely for a life disassociated from their own religious backgrounds—a story rehearsed countless times before during a century of Protestant (and Jewish) struggles with contemporary culture. To many for whom Catholicism was identical with the structures that were now vanishing or quite gone, or for whom Catholicism was bearable only in a radically reformed guise, the secular alternative seemed preferable because *their* Catholicism (either traditional or modernized) did not in fact exist. The great number of laity and clergy who have in this period left the church, for seemingly opposite reasons, shows that much of the actual disarray and weakness of the Catholic situation stems neither simply from conservative intransigence nor from liberal foolhardiness but from the steady presence of a secularistic mode of existence and thought apparently more in tune with much of modernity than is any form of Christianity, liberal or conservative. Unintentionally *aggiornamento* has meant at its deepest level the total entrance of Catholic people, in their thought-forms, norms, and styles of life, into the *secular* world of modernity. *Aggiornamento* thus poses a quite new and much deeper problem: not what form of Catholicism they will or wish to live within, but whether they wish to be Catholic or Christian at all.[22] The real problem for present-day Catholicism—dimly seen in fear, anxiety, and as a steady lure by both groups—is thus not located in the debate between ancients and moderns,

Thomists and Heideggerians, conservatives and liberals, supporters of present society or radical critics of it. Rather it is located in the deeper issue of whether *any* religious existence at all is viable, intelligible, or creative in modern life.

If, as I believe, the problem of religion itself in the secular age is in Catholicism more fundamental than the problem of newer as opposed to older forms of religious life, then three consequences follow. First, it is evident that the deepest issues for responsible reflection, with regard to theology, church structures, religious modes of existence, and the task or mission of the church in the world, are shared commonly by Catholics, Protestants, and others committed to religion: on this level of the problem we may be able to help each other. No Protestant can creatively reinterpret Catholicism in the terms of modernity, nor can a Catholic help to devise relevant forms of Protestant life. But together we can discuss how it is that modern life (as well as medieval life!) calls for a religious and Christian interpretation of individual, social, and historical existence.

Second, this means that any reformulation of Catholic doctrine and life, any "liberal" interpretation of the old forms, must deal creatively with *both* levels of the issue: that is, not only must it show how essential strains of Catholic existence may or should appear in selected modern terms, but also it must make clear how a given modernized version of Catholic life *itself* relates creatively to the structures, experiences, and needs of contemporary experience as a whole. It is not enough merely to translate Catholic categories into the terms of modern views of scripture, tradition, religious authority, theistic conceptions, Christian ethics, or ecclesiology, however radical. Rather we must continually answer as best we can the questions: Why scripture, church tradition, or religious authority *at all*? Why theism and not humanism? Why a

Christian, not a naturalistic, social ethic? Why a church and not just a community organization, secular state, or political movement? Because in the church we are all now largely ourselves "secular" in mentality and are lured by complete secularism, apologetics must become a dominant aspect of even the most confessional or intramural aspects of theological discussion. If an essential relation between even a liberal form of Catholicism and the needs and experiences of ordinary, natural life is not constantly made, then in a naturalistic age even those liberalized forms of religion, as *religion*, will seem meaningless and invalid to the great mass of formerly Catholic people, especially the youth, who now with *aggiornamento* live totally immersed in the secular world.

Third, if the largest secondary problem for Catholic reflection and life is set by the secularistic character of our culture, the seeming meaninglessness and invalidity of religious speech, and the irrelevance of religious faith to modern individual and political existence, then it follows that only a mode of Catholicism in essential touch with modern experience can cope with this level of difficulty. And obviously that implies a "liberalized" version of Catholicism set within the general terms of modern experience and thought. The difficulty with archaic forms of Catholic life was not simply that they did not fit the way the Catholic elite had been taught by modernity to think, feel, and act, though that was a problem. Rather it was that these forms, creatively in touch with life in the past, had lost all their contact with the ordinary life of Catholics in the present world, Catholics who now participate wholly in a modern experience vastly different from the cultural experience that had helped to generate those older forms of Catholic faith. Only a religion in constant relationship—intellectual, existential, moral, and political —to daily, lived experience can live in any age, and *a fortiori* can have relevance, authority, and power in an age that tends naturally to be wholly "this-worldly" in thoughts, feelings, values, anticipations, and hopes. Thus a vital form of Catholicism, as of Protestantism, is ipso facto one that has been reconceived, reformulated, and restructured in modern terms, that is to say, a liberal rather than a traditionalist version.

On the other hand, it is by the same token clear that the only form of religion that can authentically exist amidst the power and the lure of the secular is one that has a firm grasp of the reality, relevance and necessity to human existence of God. For without this grasp of the transcendent as its central element, liberalism slips unnoticed into the wholly humanistic and the secularistic. In emphasizing the essential necessity of the transcendent dimension in Christian faith—the reality or otherness of God—the conservative and the neoconservative traditions are right. What is problematic about their position is their identification of the transcendent, its retention in time and its presence in contemporary life, with the supernaturalistic structures originating in the patristic and especially the medieval periods.

This brings us to the concluding part of the introductory chapter: namely, the specific effects of the interaction of modernity and Catholicism. What precisely has the new interaction of modernity with traditional Catholicism effected in the ways Catholics now think and feel? With *aggiornamento* the Catholic people, and especially their educated elite, have moved completely within the world of modernity, "completely," that is, with regard to the way they view reality, truth, and value; in other words, their modes of fundamental feeling, thought, and deliberation. This move into the modern world has raised both the issue of *new* forms of Catholic life versus old forms, and the deeper issue of whether *any* forms of Catholic life are possible or relevant. The question now is: why did modernity seem to dissolve every traditional certainty and so pose this double issue to Catholic life? What specific effect did modernity have on the forms of traditional Catholicism when the windows were opened? Finally, what was there about modernity that caused such deep disintegration, disarray, and confusion in Catholic life?

The most general and most important answer to these questions is: the spirit of modernity has rendered vulnerable if not totally unviable the "supranaturalistic" structure of traditional Catholic thought and life. Let us first define what we mean by this "supranaturalistic structure." Inherited conceptually from the Greeks and then set into religious and Christian forms in the Middle Ages, this supernaturalism involved fundamentally a vision of two worlds, one of supernature and one of nature, and it pictured the Christian religion via its church as the divine-human mediation between them. The most general characteristic of the supernatural understanding of Christianity is, therefore, its sense of two radically distinguished realms: one natural and the other supernatural; one of the created order and the other of God; one of nature and the other of grace; one of matter, time, and space, the other of eternity; one of change, relativity, and becoming, the other of changelessness and absoluteness. The supernatural world, of course, was the realm of God and what is of God, namely, revelation, grace, and the destiny of man with God. The natural realm was the realm of nature and history, the created world in which we all here and now live on the one hand, and our created, natural, "this-worldly" values and goals on the other. The Christian religion and the church are essentially understood as providing the divinely established bridge *between* these two worlds: telling of the way the one was created and redeemed by the other, and offering the means by which persons could transcend their temporal natural state and so return to their true home in God's eternity. The church was not there so much to transform the natural as to lead it beyond itself to the supernatural, to make a bridge between these two worlds. The church thus represented the decisive *intervention* of the supernatural order into the natural order in order to guide, prepare, and ultimately translate everything in the natural order into the supernatural, which is its destiny. This intervention of supernature into nature and history is the sole basis for the power, authority, law, and mission of the church here on earth. Thus, as the place in time and space where God is uniquely at work, the church is also itself uniquely transcendent; its powers, truth, authority, laws, task, goal, and the modes of existence of its representatives are, like its source, supernatural in character—absolute, changeless, inerrant, perfect, and transcendent to nature. Its truth, enshrined in its dogmas and doctrines, is changeless and infallible; its laws are eternal and utterly authoritative; its sacraments are objectively divine and thus salvatory; its power over human destiny in absolution, remission, and anathema represents the power of God himself; its voice in teaching and ruling, through its constituted authorities or authority, is the equivalent of the divine voice in present time and space; and finally its goal, for which it has been granted those supernatural powers, is to bring souls now resident on earth to eternal peace with God. As the body of Christ, the continuation of the Incarnation, the church functions as Christ did: on the one hand as mediator between heaven and earth, and on the other with utter authority and power in his classical roles of teaching, ruling, mediating, and redeeming. Needless to say, if in this way the voice and authority of the church in doctrine, law, and rule, is directly and unequivocally *supernatural*, then the voice and authority of any autonomous individual, or even more, of any autonomous individual as a lay and therefore a "natural" man, must be subservient to the voice of the church. As God's truth towers over man's, and

as the perfection of man is obedience to God, so the
authority of the church's magisterium should rule the individual theologian, that of the bishop the individual
priest, and that of the priest the laity.

Since the church is the representative of the supernatural within nature and history, she has a two-leveled
existence and character, as did Christ in his two natures
and as does the Christian who unites with her. She is
made up of men and women, and so of natural, fallible
beings. Nevertheless, all of them have as humans a supernatural origin and destiny with God beyond this life; and
some of them, even though they are "natural" beings, are
called to embody, in the service of the church as her representatives, the supernatural life in time and space. Thus
everywhere one looked in the life of the church there
were two levels: one divine law and style of life for the
layman, another for the "religious." One sort of fulfillment
and good for the natural, "worldly" man or woman living
in the midst of family, society, and state; another sort of
fulfillment and good for the "religious," a supernatural
existence lived apart from the world and understood according to the commands of perfection in the New Testament. And, finally, one sort of truth in worldly affairs—
relative, probable, and hypothetical—and another sort of
truth in the official voice of the church and her representatives on matters of ultimate concern. Although the church
was in the world, absorbed the world in her membership,
and related herself continually to natural, relative, and
ambigious human existence in her political and economic
life, still *qua* church—in doctrine, law, forms of sacrament
and liturgy, worship, goals, and the voice of her representatives—she represented a holy and transcendent realm, a
supernatural order, a divine power and authority.

To be in her and of her, to relate to the divine through
her, meant, therefore, to move from the natural order into
that supernatural order of life that she, like an embassy on

foreign soil, represented and incarnated. To believe was to accept her supernatural truth; to communicate with her was to participate in elements divinely changed into supernatural entities; to be good was to obey her supernatural law and injunctions; to serve her vocationally was to participate in her supernatural modes of life; and, as the fullest expression of this, to be *really* Christian was to move to a level of existence with and in God himself, a level that far transcended in its substance, style, ethic, and goals, the level of obedient, faithful "nature," the worldly life of ordinary humans in the social world of history.

Correspondingly, to disobey the church or to leave her was to cut one's sole tie with the supernatural and with God; it was to be faced with a Godless and therefore a hopeless future. In representing God to man through herself and her institutional forms in idea, law, sacrament, presence, and authority, the church represented a supernatural, transnatural world; and all that she did *qua* church thus participated in the absolute, the changelessness, the perfection, the utter authority, the holiness of that supernatural order. All of this is what I mean by the "supernatural" structure, authority, and goals of traditional Catholic thought and life.

If there is one thread running through the development of the modern spirit, practically coterminous with it, it has been the cumulative critique since the Renaissance of this vision. Increasingly for the modern mentality, reality, truth, and value have shed the dualistic, two-leveled form, and have been located firmly within spatio-temporal, natural, and historical experience. The real has ceased to be primarily absolute, changeless, and unrelated, but rather it is in process, relative to other changing things, and temporal and historical in character—whether it be God, the natural world, history, or man. A true proposition, even if it concerns religious truth, is not absolute, changeless, and utterly certain; but any such proposition, or set of propositions, is probable, hypothetical, subject to test, and historically relative. Thus all religious truths and laws are relative to their cultural time and place and not supernaturally transcendent to all other human truths and obligations. Correspondingly, what is valuable is not in the first instance a supernatural level of existence for which life in the here and now is merely instrumental or preparatory; rather what is of supreme value is the fulfillment, for the self and for others, of the conditions and possibilities of natural human life in this social world and in the historical future. To live a fully *human* life, in thinking human thoughts, doing human things, creating human works, and loving other human beings, and in working in society for a more human life for all, is all that could be of value in life and therefore all that the God who sent us here could possibly ask of us. Any other vocation, even if religious, is of value only as instrumental to *that* human goal, and so itself secondary. And if that be so, the full human authenticity of ourselves, and the authenticity of our own creative emotions, intelligence, and will in relation to and for the service of others in the development of their authenticity, is the highest value to which we as humans can aspire. We live under God in a natural world and our goal as Christians is the fulfillment through grace of man's natural life in this world. Whether or not "liberation" is the best word to express this Christian aim, it does make clear the natural, social, historical, and worldly goal of much important and creative present-day Catholic theology, and consequently the vast and effective influence that secular culture has exerted on traditional Catholicism. This summary of the modern mood and perspective of life is, obviously, in many respects inexact and certainly not exhaustive. It is intended, as was the summary of traditional Catholicism above, merely to be suggestive of important trends.

The conflict between these two visions is sharp: the traditional Catholic vision of a supernatural and a natural world, and the modern vision of one, "this-worldly" process of time and becoming, and the goodness and value of the natural. And a moment's study of Catholic thought since 1962 will show how speedily and totally victorious —wherever that modern spirit was culturally predominant—the modern perspective was. In theology the sudden collapse of the intelligibility, credibility, and authority of the classical and even the neoclassical Thomist structure (the "textbook theology") is proverbial. The modern sense of the reality of process, becoming, and relatedness; of the radically empirical origin of all truths and thus the relativity and historical character of every truth so obtained, even sacred religious truths; and of the concentration of valid Christian thought, piety, and action on this life, its problems, and fulfillment, rather than on the supernatural, all these quickly demolished the old structure based on the authority of metaphysical speculation combined with scriptural and dogmatic certainties, and descriptive of a reality and a realm of existence far transcendent to the natural world of experience. And as an inevitable consequence, Catholic intellectual circles sought new modes of theological interpretation stemming from modern philosophies and social theories, and influenced by modern theologies expressive of this modern perspective.

It was, however, in the area of Catholic *existence*, not of doctrine, that in all probability the results of this conflict, and the speedy victory of modernity, were most deeply experienced. It is thus more on the level of religious existence in relation to the church and her authority than on the level of thought or theology in relation to the church's doctrine that the sudden but real disintegration of traditional Catholic life has occurred. The modern sense of the elusiveness, if not the unreality, of the super-

natural certainly has had its effect in reducing the ultimate authority of the church over her people as the sole
representative of the divine; and as a consequence her
claim in her voice and rule to embody every man's ultimate concern has been rendered fatally problematic.
Skepticism, questioning, even disobedience and departure
were rendered possible and bearable as never before for
many believing Catholics. How else can one explain the
sudden loss of the terror with which the defrocked priest,
anathematized by his church, was beheld by all Catholics,
and often by himself, even two decades ago? The current
attitudes and feelings with which laity and even priests
"drop out" of their relation to the church provide a vivid
and even shocking contrast, the loss of one entire "world"
and the gaining of another. But in my opinion the issues
of truth and its authority and of value have been the most
crucial; and here the dissolution of this understanding of
the supernatural as the central religious category has been
most clear.

In the span of a generation the absolute authority of the
church regarding truth, law, and rules of life, has suddenly vanished. Few contemporary younger Catholics
recognize *inwardly* the authority of the magisterium over
their thoughts, though in wishing to remain loyal Catholics they know they might have to deal with it politically
and even in the end perhaps submit to it. Few regard the
dogmatic statements of the church's faith as unequivocally binding on their own formulations; they are to be
sure reverenced guides, but they are not binding. Few see
the rulings of a higher hierarchical official, or even of the
holy office, over priestly duties, over their order's rules, or
over their own private style of life as a divine decree and
therefore binding inwardly on their conscience or behavior. Few feel that a cleric's views on the problems and
issues of "natural" life, though they may be derived from
sacred tradition and papal decree, have any intrinsic

claim to the truth and so to obedience on these human matters. Such churchly decrees, whether theological, ethical, or legal, derived from revelation or from the church's insight into natural law, are seen as themselves human and relative; they are relative to the time and place of their origin, and the cultural or national perspectives, the "ghetto mentality," the theology, the age, and so forth, of the men who wrote them down and the men who uttered these decrees. The sense of the historical relativity of all human statements has for many undermined completely the traditional authority of the ecclesiastical voice over faith and morals alike. The supernatural authority of the church and its representatives has disintegrated in the chill air of modern relativity and historicity.

The collapse of this authority has not occurred because certain church doctrines, papal decrees, bishops' rulings, and so on were at last found to be in error, or because certain prominent decrees were obviously "wrong" or "old-fashioned" in relation to the modern mind. This is not at all the heart of the issue, and to analyze it this way is to obscure the deeper source of the current crisis. The real issue is the *new* possibility in Catholic life of the recognition of ecclesiastical or papal error, the new possibility that a mistake from these quarters could have any meaning at all for a loyal Catholic mind. And the fact of that new possibility in turn indicates a "prethematic"* modernizing of the Catholic mind that prepared the crisis long before any of these particular decrees were conceived or

* By "prethematic" is meant a state of experience, and so of consciousness, that has a certain form (it is different from other states) but whose form has not yet been made explicit through symbols or concepts descriptive of that state. Certain common words are used to describe such prethematic states: feelings, moods, vague experiences of . . . , etc. Correspondingly, "thematic" refers to the process of *making explicit* through symbols and concepts what is latent in prethematic experience, i.e., bringing to direct reflective consciousness what was vaguely felt or undergone as a mood or tone of

appeared. If what is said officially by the church is regarded as absolute, certain, infallible, of *divine* authority,
there are then no criteria anywhere in heaven or on earth
by which that statement could be said to be wrong, and
the category of error or mistake has no possible meaning
or use in this connection. For in that case human experience, insight, and reasoning (even in their organized form
as science), all that might tell me that what the church
said was a mistake, are, if they conflict with an official
ecclesiastical decree, ipso facto *themselves* wrong. I may
not see why I am wrong, or feel that my opinion, belief,
and cognitive or value judgment are in error: they may
still *seem* right to me. But, if I believe that the holy office
speaks for God and declares me in error, then I *know* that
my philosophical, theological, or ethical view, though it
still may seem right to my mind, is in fact in error; and
consequently, in recognizing the fact of that error, I know
I must bring my mind and will into obedience to what is
clearly the truth.

It was this conviction that error is impossible, or better,
"meaningless," in relation to official ecclesiastical pronouncements, that they are supernatural in this sense,
that lay back of the real authority of the church's official
voice. And correspondingly, the new understanding, the
unthematized modernization of the Catholic mentality, in
which all such statements are felt to be historically relative, not supernatural, and so merely probable, partial,
particular, and thus themselves (as Rahner admits) even

---

consciousness. Thus, for example, there is a "prethematic" level of
consciousness of being in time, of being caused, or simply of being
that philosophy seeks to make explicit, and also a prethematic level
of religious awareness that is explicitly brought to consciousness
through religious symbols and reflectively pondered in theology. In
this way religious symbols make "thematic" what was, or could be,
"prethematic" in human experience, as that experience is qualified
by the religious dimension.

full of probable error, has undermined that ecclesiastical authority. For, if they represent human judgments, and are therefore relative, then our information, rational insight, scholarly judgments, and values can become as valid sources of knowledge of the truth and of the good as theirs. And *a fortiori* if the issue concerns an area in which "we" rather than "they" are experts (for example, for a layman as opposed to a cardinal in sexual matters, or for a scholar as opposed to a council of bishops in the meaning of scripture or of tradition itself), then clearly our judgments can in principle be more trustworthy than theirs. Consequently papal decrees on, say, birth control, in becoming for many present Catholics reflective of "Italian," "curial," and above all "medieval and monastic" perspectives rather than precise reflections of the divine perspective, can now be seen as "one-sided" or even "wrong" in relation to others' views—and they can for the first time seriously dissent. The deep unthematized but clearly present view among laity and clergy alike that the ecclesiastical voice is human rather than divine in its validity and its authority has eroded the transcendent authority of that voice and subjected it to the possibility of error—as in a former generation the same view of all truths as historical slowly became dominant in the Protestant mind and similarly for the first time subjected the formerly inerrant Bible to the possibility of factual error.

As the above illustrations show, the dissolution of supernatural authority in the areas of truth and law has frequently combined with a similar collapse of the supernatural in the area of value. So long as it was believed that a supernatural level of human existence was greater in value and closer to the deepest intentions of the divine will for men than the natural level, it was possible for men and women serenely to deny much that was natural and desirable in their own lives: their natural desires for family love and affection, sexuality, and hope for children;

and thus they could be inwardly content with the traditional ascetic forms of the clerical vocation. Not only was the law that prescribed this mode of life regarded as universal, absolute, and inwardly binding; even more important, this law embodied for the whole Catholic world a *divine* valuation of human existence and its supernatural possibilities that necessarily evoked an inward assent. The rule of celibacy might then be experienced as difficult or even as a burden; but as with all difficulties and burdens that are intrinsically related to what is believed to be a higher value, it could be borne easily through patience, obedience, fortitude, and fidelity. At the most the issue presented personal problems for particular individuals; for centuries it provoked no widespread crisis.

What has happened is that a "geological shift" in values, corresponding to the one in the view of truth, has taken place, though in this case too a prethematic modernizing of the Catholic mind and will had clearly long been at work before the crisis surfaced. Suddenly the highest values for human life were viewed "naturalistically," that is, as the fulfillment of the *natural*, and as inevitably implying the creative use of all man's natural and human powers: of thought, creativity, affection, community, organic love, and sexuality. Whether that fulfillment and perfection of the natural required a religious dimension of grace, or whether it could be achieved by man's efforts of intelligence and will alone, was still unsettled. The debate on that question separates a modern Christian understanding of man and his need for grace from modern humanism. But in either case the ultimate goal of life, religiously or humanistically understood, has become the perfection and fulfillment of our humanity in this life and in history, not the transcendence of that humanity. What had once been regarded as supernatural was now seen by a multitude of Catholics as unnatural: to allow the most important of these human powers, say that of an intimate love of other people, to atrophy; to avoid the deepest of human experiences, both the joyous and the tragic; to shut oneself off from the most crucial aspects of ordinary human living, as in the family. Such a mode of life now seemed to many to truncate, confine, impoverish, and ultimately warp the value and creativity of our given humanity. The supernatural level of life became not at all a *higher* value characterized by *deeper* joys. It became for many (though by no means for all) of less value, possibly neurotic, potentially uncreative for self, and for others it was at best a particular vocation for particular sorts of people, no longer higher and universally binding, but a special and unique way of being Christian and thus optional, as the mystical vocation always had been. Therefore the law that prescribed it as a universal obligation correspondingly became not just a difficult guide to a deeper level of living to which universal inward assent was possible; rather now it represented an anachronistic requirement extrinsic to every sense of real value and therefore potentially destructive and even tyrannical. As a sign of the collapse of the value system that supported it, celibacy was now justified "practically," as the "most useful" form for a religious vocation within the world. But such practical justifications are secondary and useless in the end; if no *intrinsic* value is seen in such a difficult mode of life, the result will be a loss of dedication to the vocation that requires it rather than acceptance of this burden as a practical requirement. And this is just what has happened. It is not, therefore, at all the sudden appearance of laziness, infidelity, and lust within the Catholic religious, male or female, that has caused the crisis of the celibate clergy, as conservatives like to say. Nor is it merely that the processes of spiritual formation were not as adequately realized in their training as in the past; rather, what is required for their vocations now seems to many to be unnatural rather than supernatural. Their

world in its values, as in its being and its truth, has become *one* world rather than *two*. Thus a rejection in their
existence of that one world, and so of its joys and its sor-
rows, is experienced as almost unbearable.

The collapse of the supernaturalistic forms of Catholicism, then, is the key to understanding both the effect of
modernity on traditional Catholicism and the current
crisis in Catholic life. For this collapse illuminates not
only each significant element of the crisis but it also clari-
fies the confusion of parties and voices on the present
Catholic scene. To many the traditional supernatural
forms of Catholicism provide the only possible historical
medium of the divine presence and therefore the only
possible structure that is validly Catholic. Some believe
that if the supernatural elements of Catholic authority,
dogma, law, and practice are eliminated, God and his
Catholic church will cease to be; and James Hitchcock
can wonder if the church will be there in the year 2000!
To others, the liberals, the divine can be present through
other more modern structures than the traditional supernaturalism; and thus they seek to translate traditional
Catholic symbols into the nonsupernaturalistic forms of
modern experience, thought, and valuations. It is here, I
believe, that the hope of Catholicism, and of Christianity,
lies in the twentieth century. Finally, there are those who,
like their conservative antagonists, identify the transcendent and the divine with the traditional supernatural
structures of the church. For them, however, Catholic
supernature and God have dissolved *together* in the face
of modernity, and *only* the secular is left. These are the
radicals: right insofar as many of them have emphasized
and in many cases implemented creatively the church's
worldly mission of protest and political and economic liberation; wrong (in my view) insofar as they find the
transcendent dimension of life and of the church as meaningless and anachronistic as are the forms in which it has

historically been expressed and mediated. The point is to
see that all three are reactions to the strong currents of
modernity, and that they are significantly *different* reactions. The conservatives and liberals are not (as radicals
feel) the same, though both value as central the continuing presence of the transcendent and the sacred; nor are
the liberals and the radicals the same, or even two stages
on the same road (as conservatives feel), though both feel
that the traditional forms have lost their mediating power
in the present age.

The task for twentieth-century Catholicism calls for the
reinterpretation of the transcendent, the sacred, and the
divine—the presence of God to men—into the worldly or
naturalistic forms of modern experience rather than in the
supernaturalistic forms of Hellenic and medieval experience. By my use here of the word "naturalism" I do not
mean to imply that the world, history, and men are all
that there is, and that religion must understand itself exhaustively in their light alone. Rather, naturalism con-
notes that our experience manifests to us one world: of
nature, history, others, and ourselves, a world of process
and becoming, of history and change, of relativity and
temporality, of autonomous, authentic selfhood, and creative community. And secondly, that the continuing and
creative ground of that world, the basis of its order and so
of our thought, the source of its meaning, healing, love,
and hope for its future, transcends that world while being
continually in creative relation to it, bringing it to God's
goal and its completion. This ground of all, this depth of
all experience, this source of order, meaning, love, healing, and hope is God. And above all, the *purpose* of what
God does and has done in that world is the redemption of
it and its natural and historical life. Such a God can be
expressed as creatively in the forms of modern experience
and thought as he was once in the forms of past thought.
To do so is necessary if our life in the modern world is to

be healed by his grace, and if the symbols of our traditional experience of his nature and redeeming work are to
be living, real, and salvific for us.

The task of Catholicism, then, is to effect a separation
of the supernaturalistic, absolutist, and extrinsic forms of
her past life from the transcendent, the sacred, and the
divine that has and will continue to permeate and uphold
her life. This implies a reinterpretation of our common
Christian symbols of God, revelation, authority, salvation,
law, and hope for the future—and their relation to historical change and becoming—in *non*supernaturalistic terms
so that they can be means of grace to our time.

Obviously the task will also involve a reinterpretation
of the *Catholic* forms of these common Christian symbols,
those traditional ecclesiastical symbols expressive of her
past claims to exclusive grace and absolute authority. The
aim of such a reinterpretation is not that she will cease to
be Catholic but that what is essentially Catholic may become alive in our own day. Can the substantive and
central reality of the *people* of God or the *ecclesia*, the
creative and essential role of *tradition*, the reality of *grace*
or of *caritas* in human relations, and the experience of
*sacramental presence* be given powerful expression and
mediation without a supernaturalistic and absolutist understanding of ecclesiastical authority and unity, dogmatic tradition, the objectivity of grace and the law, and
the goal of Christian grace? These are the fundamental
questions of the Catholic present. To me, therefore, the
primary task of Catholicism is to concentrate her vast
skill, learning, and commitment on this question of *new*
forms of Catholic life—theological, ethical, political, and
institutional—so that a new birth can take place. For on
the creative resolution of this contemporary challenge to
Catholicism depends the health of the whole church in
the immediate future.

# Chapter II

## *The Priesthood in the Modern World View*

IN FEW AREAS is the challenge to Catholicism which I discussed in the preceding chapter so crucial as in what relates to the priesthood. Nevertheless, the purpose of this discussion is not that of advancing a view of priesthood adequate to modern needs. It is, rather, to bring to our consciousness those major attitudes and convictions characteristic of modern culture and of ourselves that make priesthood difficult, its role ambiguous, and its future form infinitely unclear. This is a task I, as a Protestant, may assay, for our own Protestant traditions have been successively threatened, pummeled, picked up, and assaulted again by these same forces now for over two hundred years. Because of these forces, the Protestant minister has hardly known who he was, what he was there to do, where his authority lay, of what value any of his works were for some one hundred years. Thus we look on Catholic troubles with the genial sense of superior knowledge of a small boy who has been thoroughly whipped by the same teenager down the street. The Roman clergy has postponed its encounter with modernity until only yesterday, letting the tensions built into that encounter accumulate to gigantic force. No wonder, then, that the clergy has a traumatic feeling that suddenly everything is slipping, nothing is certain, no clues are given, and that of all vocations on earth, this one is the most confused, the most frustrated, and very probably the most useless. In the seventeenth century Milton remarked that "new presbyter is merely old priest writ large." The danger in the twentieth century is that that respectful, if hostile, remark would have to be rewritten: "New priest is just good old confused Protestant minister all over again."

We are all in trouble. The cause of our troubles—or at least of those we are aware of—is a world view that permeates our culture, and so our laity and ourselves. Our most fundamental problem of self-understanding is not that other people, the laity, do not believe in the old ways, and thus are we weak; nor is it that certain people (the Curia and certain old-fashioned bishops) are not modern and will not let us reform things accordingly, though this *is* a problem. The most fundamental problem is that we are moderns, we share this series of attitudes, and thus we are uncertain about who we are, what we are here to do, and where our authority to do it lies. Modernity is not antithetical to God's purposes—else we all be damned at once. But it makes havoc of older assumptions, structures, and goals; and it forces us to find new ways of understanding and structuring our faith, task, and profession. Most of the problems of the present church are created by modernity, but most of its glories come from the same source. When we seek to *reform* the church, to *improve* it in any way, it is to an aspect of modernity—one of these presuppositions I will allude to—that we make appeal. Were it not, to speak in a light theological vein, for the providence of God, which works in secular culture and which has created these damaging modern presuppositions, the Holy Spirit who works in the church would long since have given up the task! We owe modernity gratitude, for it creates the best in us as well as our worst problems.

I shall try to describe three major ideas characteristic of

modernity that have generated these vast changes in attitude and in turn have well nigh scuttled traditional concepts of the priesthood. In presenting them I do not mean to imply that they are *true*—only that they permeate most of our thoughts and lie back of most of our problems. A *Christian* understanding or interpretation of them is about as close to the truth as we in our age can get.

The principle of the perfection and value of nature or of the natural is by far the most significant and explosive concept in the modern spirit. I do not mean that what can be said by science is all that can ever be said, as if nature and man, the system of finite natural things, were all there is. Most of our judgments and difficulties stem from our acceptance of this principle.

The principle I refer to begins cosmically. It denies the two-story picture of the world, at the top of which there is changeless divine reality, complete and perfect in itself from all eternity, eternally self-sufficient and unrelated beyond itself—the true home of man to which he can hope to return. The modern principle affirms that natural reality as a universal system is one dynamic whole, and God is to be conceived not as a changeless reality above it, but as in continual, dynamic relation to it, as its source, ground, and goal, providing its ultimate order, meaning, and hope. Correspondingly, the value of what we call creation, both as a whole and as individual entities, appears not when these entities have left the natural sphere for the divine realm, but when, united to the divine ground, they achieve their own intrinsic natural perfection. In being its natural self, realizing its own perfections in its own natural context, each creature gains its goal. Thus are nature in general, and especially man's nature, conceived to have their real home *here*, in space and time and in this natural and historical context. Correspondingly, their value, *telos*, and goal, is to fulfill their natural being—not to achieve any higher level of existence above, beyond, and different from that natural level of being. There is no separate realm more significant than this natural realm. In the divine intention, therefore, our eternal destiny is not such as to subordinate or render insignificant or of less value our present "natural" destiny in this world of humans and society. And consequently there are no supernatural virtues that crowd out and replace natural virtues. Above all we find uncomfortable the thought that such a separated ultimate goal determines our entire present life and thus sets for us here standards of truth, value, and activity that conflict with our natural truth and homely human values.

While in faith we may believe that the divine reality transcends nature, still, for us the divine is not conceivable as another realm but solely as the source of created life here and now; and for us, even Christians, *this* life is our sole context and its perfection our sole goal. Grace for us in truth perfects nature, but (and here is the important point) it does not supersede nature or raise it to a further, nonnatural level. We all tacitly believe we are called as Christians to fulfill our *humanity*, not to transcend it; and further, as ministers, our task is not so much to lead people to another sphere but to help them to fulfill their natural life here, to increase their human well-being, personal depth, communal love, and material and emotional security. The relevant evils to be overcome are those issues around us here and now, of social injustice and justice, of war and peace, and not a hell threatening hereafter. Consequently even our religious goals and the relevant heavenly Kingdom are here and now. This is our relevant context, and religion, grace, even God, if they are to be relevant and real to us, must make a difference in this context, in society, in history, and among men. Whatever our theological lingo, the two-story universe has disappeared in our actual judgments: religion turns toward *this* life for its tasks, authority, standards, and goals. The celebration of nature and of history as our home, the seat of our authority, and the sole locus of our values is what I mean by this principle—and it has had infinite repercussions.

Most of us affirm this principle at a deep visceral level, though we may be somewhat disturbed when we hear it spelled out theologically, for then the conflict with traditional views and values becomes plain. In any case, if relevant reality is a whole and the two-story world has vanished, then the seat of all authority and value lies here among space-time events. This means that religious truth, if it is relevant, meaningful, and valid for us, cannot claim for us any heavenly authority, as if it had just been sent down from the upper story. Rather, it must justify itself in relation to general or universal experience, and the general canons of reason, including scientific reason of all sorts, and also existential as well as objectifying reason. We are not inclined to recognize as true theological propositions that are not so justified and that merely claim a divine authority for themselves. No religious doctrine or traditional opinion that flies in the face of recognized scientific data can long be held once this mood is accepted —as recent discussions of population problems have demonstrated. Even Father Rahner has found he cannot hold on to an anthropological Adam in the face of anthropologist Leakey and his African gorge. And no religious doctrine that fails to have relevance or meaning for us in our present experience will be long discussed among us.

Finally, nowhere in Catholic studies is there any doubt about the legitimacy of the application of critical historical methods to even the most sacred truths, concerning, for example, the scriptural materials, the life of the early church, and the development of dogma and praxis. Authority for all of us has no locus except here in this world, in present experience; and consequently the authorities we recognize must be generated out of experience itself. Generally this means that experience rationally and objectively dealt with is for us the supreme criterion, as our use and acceptance of scientific and historical methods show. If we do claim that theological language is more than science, that it is "existential" or "symbolic" in character, then we base the claim on the character of our experience, and not merely on authority. For our time no hierarchy, tradition, or set of dogmas enjoys a special status outside this wholeness of natural reality on which another, qualitatively different, sort of authority might be based—as was certainly the case only a few years ago. Religious truth has joined the ranks of probable and partial secular truth—and the priest is no longer, like an officer entering from headquarters, reporting a heavenly truth to the troops in the trenches. All of this we accept and use as arguments against the conservative hierarchy. But it leaves us ambiguous as priests about what sort of truth, aside from our own personal opinions, and that of other "liberals," we ourselves speak for.

Much more explosive is this principle with regard to value, to the model of the perfection of human life. If for us authority is located here, then even more *value* is here as well. The goal of Christian faith, then, is not to transcend this life into another, into a supernatural level characterized by a sharing in the divine life that abrogates or absorbs natural life; for the perfection of nature is the sole value. We have no wish to be *aufgehoben* above our natural humanity, nor do we believe it possible. Correspondingly, the standards by which we judge moral good and evil, personal health and illness, and social justice and injustice, are the standards of the fullness of natural humanity and not standards related to the requirements of a level beyond the natural.

The revolutionary results of this principle of modernity, commonly accepted by most of us, can be seen in relation to two of the most controversial ethical issues of current Catholic life: birth control and celibacy. It is, first of all, on the basis of this principle that Catholic arguments *against* the traditional view of birth control have been mounted. For only when the natural life of man, with regard to the sexual relations of man and wife, the health and good prospects of children, and the welfare of an exploding population as a whole, is taken as the supreme value, do the older principles seem dubious or even immoral, untrue as aspects of a "natural law." Ironically the newer principle of natural value has here come into conflict with an ancient principle of natural law.

Secondly, with regard to celibacy, if man's goal is to fulfill his human nature, rather than to transcend it, and if it is recognized that man is an organic, instinctive, sexual, personal, and communal being, then the perfection of man, the highest level of life that can be conceived, is the unity of these natural capacities and powers and not the elimination of any of them. This new principle for evaluating man, including priestly man, completely changes assessments of celibacy and accounts for the sudden Catholic questioning of it. For if no higher value is seen than the perfecting of our natural humanity, then another mode of life—for example the celibate—is not chosen because it is higher, closer to a divine level of life; it is valued only insofar as it seems to serve the natural needs of others in the fulfillment of their humanity here and now. The celibate sacrifices his full humanity so that others may more easily achieve theirs. If in turn the value of this service were to be doubted, then the legitimacy of celibacy would itself inevitably be doubted—and this is, I suspect, what has happened. Also the reasons given for this doubt illustrate the principle here cited: celibacy is currently questioned because, it is argued, it may be damaging to the total personality, because it may repress one central aspect of man's personal being, his sexuality;

or because it is said to deprive him of the most important aspect of personal community and love, the sexual love and companionship of marriage. In all these cases the questioning arises because it is felt to prevent the full development of natural humanity. In such arguments, natural humanity is—however defined—accepted as the norm of a Christian view of man and its perfection as the goal of Christian grace.

Furthermore, once the perfection of the natural is the recognized goal, a supernatural level of life takes on negativity; it is suspected of being restrictive, repressive, of distorting the natural—instead of providing the basis for its perfection and completion. Chastisement of the flesh is now looked on by many as neurosis; a supernatural obedience that becomes second nature as bloodless and inhuman. For this mood the classical supernatural virtues—faith, hope, and love—are reinterpreted: insofar as they remain as central (and they should) they are seen solely as the principles by which the natural is perfected and fulfilled, not principles by which it is transcended. Faith is now the basis of man's humanity and so its possession the condition of being fully human; love is the fulfillment of the organic, communal life of man in family and in society; and hope is directed at a human well-being in the new historical world of the future.

Finally, many other rather radical revisions of theology are implied here. As the ground of the present and the natural rather than the supernatural goal for the hereafter, God here is no longer the divinely changeless *object* of our religious concentration, and especially, if making him that object lessens concern with man and community. At best God is here the source and ground of the fulfillment in the present and future of personal and social possibilities. To be real for us and to be able to be experienced by us, the divine must be creative of life here, the dynamic source and ground of what we are, whose purpose it is that we be what we are; and thus a God immanent in all creative things, related to all human and cultural concerns, and intent not on heaven but on a better world. Correspondingly, I suspect the present church really knows no certain function except that of ministering in this life to redeem the ills of men: it is the servant church. Once the vast cosmic duality of supernature and nature, and its results—the ethical duality of this life and the next, a supernatural life of grace and a natural life of earth—are gone, the priesthood and the church become what most of us agree they should be: not embassies arranging visas to another world, but ministering parts of our social and historical existence.

Clearly, if reality is a whole and the natural is its goal, this does not mean atheism, that the transcendent depths of life are washed away, that mystery does not remain in relation to these depths, that our separation from them— and so from our own nature as man—is not possible, and that grace is not needed to reunite us to the divine and to our own true selves. Theology takes a new form in the new world of naturalism; it does not die. And it is in this new context that the fundamental theological questions of our time reveal themselves. If nature is a whole, who or what is God? If our only authorities are experience and reason, how is religious truth possible? If values are human and natural, what is the purpose of religion? Correspondingly, with regard to the priestly vocation, several questions arise. If authority is human, on what grounds can a priest claim to possess and state the truth for all men—or even the truth interesting to some? If grace is the perfection of nature, why is sacramental or religious grace needed at all, and why does the priest of all people have any special relation to it? On the assumption that a clergyman is good for any community, what does his ordination add if nature is thus supreme? One can hear the layman asking: "A priest may be privy to many heavenly counsels, but am not I as a layman far closer to nature, and human nature, than he?" These questions stem from this fundamental principle of modern life: the wholeness and value of natural, created life.

The second basic concept characteristic of modernity, and so a presupposition that lies back of all our theological and religious reactions, is the sense of the relativity of all things to one another. This is clearly related to the first principle: the wholeness of the natural system of which we are a part implies the relatedness of everything in the natural and historical context. Nothing intervenes from outside with a totally different level of being, mode of functioning, or quality of authority; or, more pertinently, nothing in history is absolute, timeless, universal in character and authority. No documents, concepts, laws, or propositions promulgated by the greatest authorities are absolute, divine, unchallengeable. Everything we encounter in history, every person in whatever role, every page of writing, and every opinion has *some* value, but none has *absolute* value. Consider medieval farming machinery, Renaissance banking habits, and Victorian sexual rules: here we know that everything is relative to its context, and thus that a past context is alien and irrelevant to us, not an authority over us. It is harder to see this in religious matters. Still, even Jesus, most moderns believe, shared the Judaic consciousness of the first century; and thus, whatever we may wish to affirm theologically of his deity, few modern theologians would deny that he might well have been in error about many things that we know now. In the same way, we recognize that sacred scripture is filled with relative points of view: a Deuteronomic source, a second Isaianic viewpoint, Pauline, Mattheian, and Johannine traditions. The Bible for modern criticism is a congeries of relative viewpoints, not a proclaimer of a single absolute one. We also know that the historic creeds

reflect a "Greek" context in their conceptuality, and therefore can hardly serve as more than pointers to modern
theological solutions, not as authorities over them. And as
a consequence, every present theological statement, by
pope, curia, or priest, has relativity of time and place built
right into it: it reflects its time, and thus, as Karl Rahner
says, it probably suffers from crypto-heresy. In short, no
matter how we may define it today, magisterial authority
is regarded as historically relative, in part truth but in
part error. And so for our age no heirarchical authority
that understands itself as unchallengeable can justify itself to us. All views in history are now for us opinions or
attitudes, proposals for our consideration, not declarations
that we must accept. We know that even popes can make
mistakes, that bishops can be merely foolish or stubborn.
This deep sense of the historical relativity of all aspects of
the church's life is obviously presupposed in every negative reaction to any recent papal encyclical, seeing it as
"conservative," "curial in origin," "stemming from the Italian social situation," and so forth. With all due respect,
such reactions clearly regard the encyclical as a product,
at least in part, of its particular historical and social locus,
and not a document transcending all particular stand-
points and thus claiming an absolute and universal validity. This principle of relativity, combined with the new
evaluation of our natural humanity and its needs, makes
possible the appearance of the present dissenting liberal
group within Catholicism as a whole. The size of the liberal group in Europe and the United States is precisely
coterminous with the cultural scope of this principle aspect of modernity—as any person who speaks of the
"problem" of an Italianate hierarchy in relation to the rest
of the Catholic world clearly understands.

Let us note that this principle that, once recognized
and enacted, has freed the priest from the hierarchy
above him at the same time also increases the problems of

the priest's self-understanding. Historically he has been understood as a "mediator," one who mediates to the people an absolute truth and law, expressed through the authoritative judgments of the church. But if there *is* no absolute doctrine, nothing that is not relative to time, place, and social locus, then what does he mediate in the realm of ideas or of law? As he realizes uneasily, there is no *real* role or vocation as mediator of that which is relative: what, then, is the purpose and use of *mediating* thirteenth-century views, Italian judgments, or verdicts on the family life of childless males? He either keeps quiet, as having no more to say than anyone else; or he finds himself embarked uneasily on the task of *interpreting* life for his situation and locus rather than mediating an absolute answer that has been given to him. Thus are liturgy reworked for the people, doctrines spelled out in new forms in *their* terms, law reconceived in the context of *their* needs and standards. But the priest wonders uncomfortably, where does *he* get the authority to do this constructive, creative job of interpreting life and morals to his people? Is it *this* power that was given him by his ordination, or communicated to him by his training? Why should his people pay attention if it is his creativity that has produced what he says? Can there, therefore, *be* a priesthood if there is nothing absolute and given to mediate in doctrine and law, and no transcendent authority latent in the acts of mediation? Is there not simply the role of friend, counselor, village philosopher, succeeding by means of his brains and personality—precisely the somewhat "soupy" mixture that characterizes the Protestant pastor?

Having stated so bluntly the threatening implications of this sense of relativity, let us not overlook the vast positive results of that principle in our cultural and religious life. Unquestionably the sense of the relativity of all historical institutions, social structures, and individual roles has

been the creative basis for democracy, individual conscience, the ideal of self-determination, and confidence in
an open future. Only when the absolute structures, authorities, and requirements of life were gone—divinely
appointed kings, divinely founded class structures, divinely sponsored vocations—were men free in their own
minds to *transform* these institutions and social structures.
When institutions were seen to be relative, historically
created, for the first time deliberate social reform became
conceivable; when institutional authorities were seen to
be relative, created by history and not by God, then correspondingly men realized that they were free to unseat
them and choose others in their place. When no voice has
the full truth, suddenly all are felt to be in part right, and
in part wrong; and the value of the free expression of any
opinion becomes evident. Only when no one speaks for
God does error begin to have rights in the public scene.
Above all, the sense of the relativity of every Christian
communion has made possible the ecumenical movement.
When there was an absolute truth to be had, you can be
sure each of our churches would claim to have it! The
possibility that each communion will feel mutual respect
toward and need for the others amidst real disagreement
lies in their common recognition of the relativity of the
perspectives from which they each look at the Christ, at
God, and at his call to us. Tolerance is the initial historical
and social requirement for the possibility of an actual
community of love; for no love can arise among self-
determining persons without respect and forbearance, and
those are not possible without tolerance. Thus the possibility of a community of love depends on some sense of
the relativity of each position in the community—that
there are many who are of Paul and many of Apollos, but
only one Christ.

It would seem, then, that the presupposition of historical relativism, so destructive of the traditional dogmas,

the hierarchy, and the law of the church, and so threatening to the vocation of the priest, is a necessary condition for the realization of Christianity. This assertion may seem fairly strong, but we should recall that love *does* involve respect for the neighbor and thus a relativizing of one's own opinion when it differs from his. Quite possibly, therefore, if we understand the purpose of the Incarnation as the gift of the possibility of loving one another in historical community—not the gift of absolute doctrine or propositions leading to a supernatural level of life—we shall be able to see in this modern principle something creative for our Christian life, a strange preparation, if not for the Gospel, at least perhaps for its historical enactment. This insight may illustrate once again the mysterious interlocking of the work of providence which lies back of our secular ideas and the development of modernity, and the divine redemption that resulted in the Christ. For as the development of the idea of the wholeness of natural life has turned the church outward in new ways to serve the world, so the development of the relativity of all historical life has created the possibility of understanding in a more concrete way what a community of love is like, and how it may become historically possible.

The first principle was the wholeness and potential completeness of natural reality; the second was the relativity of all things historical. And now the third: the necessity and the right of autonomy or self-determination if man is to be man. The interrelations of these three concepts is instructive. Humanity is characterized by rationality and freedom, by the need for the self's own affirmation of whatever truth that self holds, and of the self's free participation in whatever significant acts that self undertakes. If the good of life is the fulfillment of this natural humanity as *self*-determining and therefore personal, then no other realm transcendent to a man's reason and will can totally determine his life—no ground is given for a truth and a law for him that does not spring from the needs and capacities of his own natural human nature. And if all human authorities are relative, it follows for any human among humans, that only *his* mind, only *his* conscience, and *his* will can have ultimate authority for him. Autonomy is the necessary consequence of the concept that it is in becoming fully human, and therefore personal, free, and self-determining, that we fulfill ourselves; and a parallel concept is that since no man speaks directly for God or for all mankind, each man in the end must speak and determine his acts for himself.

There is probably no principle so deeply ingrained in our cultural life, nor any so precariously maintained. Its history is the history of the modern spirit, or, as Hegel said, it is the history of the development of autonomous freedom that is the clue to the meaning of history itself. Certainly it is commonly accepted that the forced holding, or even the listless or conventional holding, of a correct doctrine is religiously useless; that a resentful obedience to a law is morally sterile, and that a rote-like participation in the sacraments, meaningless. Personal and free participation in what we do—be it loving, praying, or voting—and personal affirmation of what we say and believe—be it about politics, morals, or God—are necessary if man is to be man, if the community he lives in is to be healthy, and if the church is to be the church. Autonomy has become one of the basic principles by which we understand the church and religion, and by which we judge other views as valid or invalid.

This affirmation of autonomy has in turn had a fundamental effect on the traditional structures of church life and the priesthood. If, as I believe is the case, what we might call the "sacrality of the person" in his free inwardness and self-determination is one of the implications of this principle of autonomy, then surely the whole author-

ity, tenor, and purpose of canon law and of penance is
reversed. Previously, the law had objective divine authority; it specified the unalterable conditions through which
man could be fulfilled in his eternal destiny, and thus it
defined the shape of his autonomy, the form that his freedom gave to his life. But if autonomy, *self*-determination,
is now regarded as a sacred principle, this objective traditional format will itself become relative and meaningless,
even destructive, and it will be reshaped in a new and
very different direction. Now the function of the law, and
thus the role of the priest as counselor and confessor, is
that of building up the autonomous powers of the person,
in making proposals for the self-direction of his life, in
providing "wisdom" in the achievement of his personal
being.

Moreover, taking the principle one step further, if the
fulfillment of personal being is thus the goal of penance,
then clearly the person alone—on the principle of autonomy—must decide for and achieve the fulfillment of that
being. Can the priest tell the person how to be himself, or
even give to him the power to become it? Thus not only is
canon law reshaped into "wisdom" directed at personal
fulfillment, but also the person himself replaces the priest
as the final judge with regard to his own spiritual health,
i.e., as to what law applies and as to whether the law and
its rule really help in this case. The priest becomes at best
an advisor and counselor in man's personal quest for fulfillment: he is certainly not the direct mediator of an unquestionable divine law and divine grace to the individual. I am sure each priest has noted how rarely he himself
feels inwardly competent—though he may know the law
very well—to say with authority: "This is wrong." But he
may be unconscious of the basis of this new uncertainty.
It lies in the new principle, subconsciously affirmed by the
priest and by his confessee, that the value involved in
penance, as in most of the activities of religion, is the

fulfillment of the autonomous personal being of each and by each, where only the confessee can be the final human judge, not the confessor. That value does not lie, as it once did, in making one ready to appear before the throne of grace, for which appearance objective rules of life, unchallengeable by our autonomy, were given. In the new quest the priest is advisor, counselor, and friend, not legislator and judge.

Perhaps the most familiar expression of this new principle of autonomy in contemporary Catholic life is in terms of the now oft-repeated sacrality of individual conscience. I can only do what *I* think is right: every other course, whoever determines it for me, is immoral rather than moral, repressive rather than creative—and probably no nearer to the objective moral truth, whatever that may be. This principle has been appearing more and more frequently in Catholic ethical writing. It expresses vividly the new orientation toward value. If the point of life and the goal of religion is to get us to another life whose rules we do not know by nature but which we must follow or be left out, then an objective law and an authoritative mediation on the part of the priest is necessary and intelligible. In this context individual conscience, though good in itself, has little value or authority, for it can be so easily wrong in relation to these objective rules! But if the person is the locus of value, everything is reversed. Only what builds up personal being in ourselves and in others is now good; the law has lost its objectivity over against the person, and only what destroys persons is bad. Further, only if a man determines autonomously his own moral life is he moral and personal in that life, that is, is the goal of religion achieved; ergo, the sacrality of his individual conscience follows directly from this modern concentration on the value of natural, personal, communal life. We have noted how this changes the role of the priest: no longer does he mediate to people an objective law in relation to

which their individual conscience alone appears, a law
that shapes and determines conscience. Now persons are
immanently the source of the moral law for themselves,
since morality has as its goal the achievement of their
personal being in community, their natural humanity.
Religion is an important, even necessary, basis for such
personal and social growth. But religion is there as a
framework for this personal achievement; it does not provide goals, laws, and authorities that transcend and subvert this as the primary goal. Thus the priest is the helper
and advisor on the road, essential only because of the
wisdom embodied in this tradition, because of his *caritas*
for the problems and sufferings of others, and because
through Word and Sacrament alone can the individual
attain the level of faith and commitment that makes this
healing process possible. There is here little authority and
practically no moral objectivity but possibly new and
greater opportunities for real ministry.

It need hardly be added that this concern for personal
fulfillment as the goal of the priest's ministry completely
transforms his role in reflection to social problems. No
longer does he pluck individual brands from the burning
and leave the social fire alight. His role is to help recreate
humanity here and now, and that means to subvert and
refashion within his means the structures of our common
life that determine, for good or ill, whether men and
women can have personal fulfillment or not. His ministry
is the upbuilding of humanity and the reshaping of the
secular city.

Clearly this principle of autonomy in the area of truth
is equally subversive of traditional hierarchical authorities. Only that which a man can himself affirm to be true
can have religious value for him. Again, objective doctrine, like objective law, loses its value and authority in
itself, and becomes a proposal to the churches for their
consideration. No modern theologian, or set of them, or

council of bishops—even in Rome—can in a definitive
fashion tell the people in the churches what Christian
truth is. For what they too say will be relative; and even if
it were not so, such objective truth has no religious value
until it is affirmed by the people because it convinces
them and they believe it—not because it is officially
stated. As a theologian one can only have the *intention* of
expressing validly the faith for our time, and proposing it
to the consciences of the people of God for their faithful
consideration, for only what they believe is of use to
them. Thus merely to tell people what they *should* believe, even if stated correctly, is religiously useless. Truth
is not maintained in the church by authoritative and
magisterial pronouncements; nor is it through the possession of correct creeds that the church has the truth. Only
if it is so presented that it becomes intelligible, meaningful, and valid for the people of the church who hear it is
there truth within the church. Thus the form of theological argument changes radically. No longer is the argument a deductive proof of the rightness and authority of
the statement, a deduction from recognized authorities
leading to a declared or pronounced conclusion, which is
then presented as a consequence to be believed by the
hearer. Rather the argument moves toward the experience
of the hearer, his experience as a human among humans,
and seeks to illumine that experience with the aid of
Christian symbols. In this way the anxieties and mysteries
of his life are clarified and healed, and the hearer himself
is enlightened and so convinced. Theology is a proposal
for the deliberation of the church in its time; it proposes
an interpretation of Christian symbols as true for us, and
asks the church as a whole, and the theological community in particular, to ponder this interpretation, criticize,
and affirm, refashion, or refuse it. This is, granting relativity and individual conscience, all that theology can ever
be. This is a new and difficult role for theology, and so

also for the priest as theologian, far more precarious and less authoritative than when it was a scientific deduction from authoritative truths—but far more a ministry to men and women and to their time!

We are left with endless questions, but two must be asked. If individual conscience is so crucial to the truth, what happens to the magisterium? Or, to put this question theologically, in this situation for which individual conscience has a sacral character, where is the locus of the Holy Spirit as the spirit of truth, and how is error to be avoided in the church if no one voice speaks for God? The principle of natural value led to a reinterpretation of God from a transcendent changelessness to a dynamic and immanent relatedness, and the principle of relativity assisted in a reinterpretation of the Incarnation as the gift of the community of love: in conclusion let me suggest that the principle of autonomy makes possible a reinterpretation of the locus of the Holy Spirit as the bearer of truth in the church. If it is an authoritative hierarchy that bears the holy truth in the church, it follows that the truth is contained and preserved in its pronouncements—and to be "in the truth," Sören Kierkegaard would say, is to accept those pronouncements. In such a situation an authoritative magisterium, a teaching authority representing this hierarchy, guaranteeing the validity of its pronouncements, makes sense. The only problem today is that very few of us believe any of that; one reason is the principle of relativity; and another is that our belief in the religious necessity of an autonomous individual conscience makes this an inconceivable idea—from, I believe, Karl Rahner right on leftwards. But if the magisterium is so radically reinterpreted as almost to fade from existence as a determining authority over what can and should be said in the church, where is the locus of the Holy Spirit and how is the truth to be guaranteed in the church?

The answer has now begun to be clarified for the first

time, thanks to these modern principles. The locus of the
Holy Spirit as the bearer of Christian truth *is* in the
church, which is the people of God. It resides, therefore,
in the informed minds and the individual consciences of
the members of the church, not solely in the hierarchy.
Our distinction from the hierarchy as theologians and
priests is *vocational* and not *essential* or *religious*—
matters of training and concentration—not matters of
religion, piety, or fidelty. Theological truth, therefore, is
gained when the church, which is the people, compre-
hends, believes, and affirms its faith—not when correct
doctrine is pronounced by authorities, even if it were capable of being so pronounced. But, we ask, granted that the
hierarchy can be wrong, is it not even more true that the
congregation, the people of the church, can be wrong too?
Is there not here in the congregation an infinite variety of
opinion, and so an infinite possibility of error, unless these
opinions are controlled? Is not dangerous heresy almost
unavoidable? Is not the abandonment of fundamental
symbols possible if the masses of the people are regarded
as the bearers of the truth with no external authority
there to direct their wayward belief? Of course, that is the
point of the doctrine of the Holy Spirit and why we say
we *believe* in the Holy Spirit. We men and women as a
hierarchy, as a class of theologians, or as a people, cannot
guarantee the truth. The Holy Spirit at work in the
church alone can do this, and we must trust him and not
try to usurp his role. The way he works in us must be
reconceived; and we have said he works not through
authority, but through individual conscience in all its
variety.

Variety of opinion is the sole human way of achieving
the truth: it respects individual conscience, and it bal-
ances the relativity of each position with the correction of
other points of view. In effect, the ecumenical movement
has provided the *new* locus for the Holy Spirit and for our

faith in the continuity of Christian truth. For the errors of each viewpoint and the lacks of each communion are balanced by the wisdom and the strength of the others. Out of this discussion encompassing all points of view in the whole church such truth as is granted to us will emerge as Christian men and women listen, comprehend, assent, or correct one another—provided that the entire church joins in the discussion. Those views that the church does not accept will slowly recede in importance; those that it finds timely, relevant, and valid will be creatively significant in their own time. There is no other way that we in this historical life can more closely approximate, maintain, or guarantee the truth; and to believe that this mode of fidelity through freedom will succeed is to believe in the continuing presence of the Holy Spirit in the life of the whole church. This is how the Holy Spirit works through individual consciences, and it is our sole hope for the future.

First, this understanding of the continuing presence and work of the Holy Spirit in and through our free and therefore varied and often conflicting viewpoints is better expressed in the word "indefectable"—so eloquently defended by Hans Küng—than it is by the more traditional word "infallible." For with historical men truth is possessed over time more through a continuing process of discussion among relative points of view than through the promulgation of apodictically certain statements. Thus truth, if present at all, is embodied in this *process* of movement toward the truth, a movement which proceeds through relative truths and relative errors; it is not there enshrined whole and entire in any one statement or series of statements. Therefore, while no one "truth" is itself infallible, the process, as a continual (and divinely guided) approximation to the truth is surely "indefectable." Unless some members of the church are regarded as transcending (through grace) the human condition of relativity, such indefectability of a serious, open process of discussion is the closest to the divine, infallible truth as men in time can come.

Second, this in turn does not at all mean that with regard to the question of truth there is no creative role for hierarchy or magisterium, however either one may be institutionally defined. For it is useful, even necessary, for the truth, *as it can be known and formulated by the church*, to be stated as clearly and relevantly as possible. This is so intramurally for the purposes of preaching, catechism, teaching and guidance, and to provide a center and focus for creative theological discussion; and it is so extramurally in order to furnish a way of making the church's considered views known to the world at large. But all such "authoritative" views are themselves human and relative to their time and place. Thus logically they cannot be an *absolute* over either individual belief or theological formulation; nor can they be regarded as irrevocable and incorrigible, especially if theology is to pursue its task of creative reformulation on all important issues of faith and life. The magisterium of the church *can* represent (and has, to my mind, in fact represented) the "official" mind of the church at a given time, the dominant and central point of view of the whole community formulating for its time what the sanctioned representatives of the church take to be her position on the important matters of her life. Such a role in the community of faith is crucial, as are all other teaching and pastoral roles. But, as the next chapters explain, it is a *human* role, guided, corrected, and alone made indefectable by the Holy Spirit.

# Chapter III

*Symbols and
Theology*

IN THE FOLLOWING CHAPTERS I shall be speaking of theological understanding, its sources, elements, modes of comprehension or meaning, and the ground of assent to its truth. My aim will be to interpret theological understanding so that it will be intelligible in terms of modern experience and modern concepts of meaning and truth, and yet also an adequate and, hopefully, compelling reflective vehicle for the traditional claims of the Catholic tradition.

In any such attempt to clarify the structure of Christian theology, we quickly encounter several elements or levels of religious discourse: first, *stories* about events in history and God's part in them arising from the oral and the scriptural inheritance proclaimed and taught by the church; second, reflection on these stories resulting in *doctrines* that became increasingly philosophical in form and led to severe controversies; third, the appearance of *dogmas* as codified, sanctified, and authoritative expressions of the whole church's definitive interpretation of her inheritance of belief and reflection upon it; fourth, more philosophical elaboration of these dogmas into traditional church *theology*. Clearly, one of the main issues for contemporary Catholicism concerns the status—the meaningfulness and validity in the light of modern ways of thinking—of precisely this cumulative deposit of traditional doctrine, dogma, and theology, that has defined Catholic belief. Modern science and historical inquiry have increasingly challenged the historical validity and the inherent authority of many of the "stories" (about the Hebrews, Jesus, and the disciples) seemingly intrinsic to our faith; modern canons of knowing have questioned the very possibility of any changeless and supremely authoritative doctrines or dogmas. The modern sense of historical relativity has doubted the authority of past dogmatic and doctrinal formulations, however sacrosanct or important; and changes in modern sensibilities and thought forms have found anachronistic and thus irrelevant the philosophical and theological elaborations of these dogmas generated in another age. If, then, the forms in which Christian belief has been mediated to us are under such essential attack, how is the traditional basis of our faith to be expressed in modern terms that are intelligible, meaningful, and true to us?

In order to answer this question, I shall seek to comprehend this inheritance of belief and its reflective expression in terms of a set of categories slightly different from the traditional set (i.e., stories, doctrines, dogmas, and definitive church theology): namely, stories, "myths," and symbols on the one hand, and scientific and philosophical analysis on the other. A contemporary Christian theology is a synthesis of these elements, the first (stories and symbols) traditional and the second (scientific and philosophical analysis) contemporary. The purpose is to show the role of each of these elements in a viable modern theology and something of their interrelations. The most useful place to begin is with the dialectic between stories and analysis; that is, understanding theologically in terms of the recitation of past events and through the analysis and uncovering of present structures. For both are essential to theology. Clearly here we are touching on the much-debated issue of history and "myth" on the one hand, and their relation to science and philosophy on the other.

Study of the historical development of man's reflection shows that human understanding begins with stories. When man first sought to understand the structures—environmental, social, political, and moral—within which he found himself living, he told stories about their establishment, about the gods, or the great heroes who founded these structures. These are what we generally call "myths," though the men who told them would not have thought of them that way. They appear in every early culture expressing in verbal and story form the "world" in which the culture lived. Myths thus performed several functions basic to man's existence: they shaped the horizon of man's experience by giving verbal and conceptual structure to the central realities, natural and social, in which he found himself; they made legitimate his social and political world and his relation to nature by tracing both back to their divine foundations; they explained and therefore made bearable the painful and tragic aspects of his experience and gave him grounds for hope in the conquest of these evils; and they were the source for his normative judgments about his society, his fellows, and himself.

In linguistic form these myths were "stories," that is, they concerned themselves with the recitation of events in the past and therefore they used historical language. They were, however, unusual stories, or, rather, stories of unusual events. For they depicted not merely an ordinary occurrence *within* the structures of present existence, but the sacred occurrences in which these structures came to be. Although their language was the language of actors and of actions in space and time, historical language, the content of the myths concerned the founding of the world in which all ordinary action takes place. These stories or myths therefore had a *transcendent* referent: a superhuman or divine actor who created, intervened in, or appeared within the ordinary sequence of events. Knowledge of these mighty events and of the actor or actors who accomplished them was not "ordinary knowledge," achieved merely by examining the present scene, however closely. It came through the sacred tradition recited by those who knew, a tradition ultimately inscribed in sacred texts, an avenue later to be called revelation.

In the long development of man's cultural life since earliest times, understanding through such stories or myths has gradually been replaced by another mode of understanding—that of analysis of the structures available to *present* experience and to present inquiry. First there appeared the inquiries of speculative philosophy, and then more and more in the modern period the empirical analysis called science. One of the most fundamental problems for Christian theology of all sorts in our time has been whether a mythical understanding is possible or relevant in a culture whose modes of knowing and comprehending are dominated by the analysis available to present, and so shareable and testable, experience. Ironically, as Auguste Comte rightly predicted, both theological and speculative understanding live a precarious life in our present world where empirical analysis rules as almost the sole veridical form of knowing.

Despite all the pressures in our culture to dispense with mythical language in theology, however, theology is intrinsically dependent upon and characterized by the story form. It cannot, without fatal results, be collapsed into purely metaphysical or ontological language, nor can it be reduced to scientific discourse. When it does collapse—when the most fundamental and determinative forms of theological speech are either metaphysical or scientific in form—then theology ceases to perform its proper function. The transcendent horizon and its relation to man's whole existence is no longer what theology talks about, the ultimate that makes man man is no longer what it names; and so other myths replace it as thematizing the real horizon of man's world and expressing his real confidence for his present and future life. Religious symbols, which structure the ultimate horizon in which man lives and whose essential meanings in our tradition have a "story" form, call in each age for theological and philosophical elaborations or elucidation if they are to become meaningful, intelligible, and valid to the men of that age; they do not call for replacement by philosophical conceptuality. Philosophy thus has a hermeneutical, not a magisterial, role in relation to fundamental religious symbols. In theology, therefore, understanding through analysis explicates; it does not transcend, determine, or replace our religious understanding through stories. More specifically, there are three reasons why understanding through stories, the language of myth or symbol, must characterize Christian theology at its best.

1. All we can know about God is through his *activity* in us, on us, and on our world, that is, in terms of the continuum of our experience in the world of process, change, and time. To be sure, it is difficult enough to know anything ultimate about either that world of becoming or of God's role in it; theology is difficult inquiry, and the divine object of theology infinitely elusive. But this is all the theology we could know in any case. On the one hand, our modern understanding of revelation as lacking any absolute, propositional assertions and as devoid of objective "information" about God as he is in himself and, on the other, our contemporary skepticism concerning speculation that might ascend beyond the range of immediate experience and inform us through that route of the essential divine nature as he is in himself mean together that both classical ways of knowing God *quoad se* are closed to us, or appear to us to be more compounded of our speculative fancies than of his actuality. If we are to know God

at all, it is as he impinges on our experience *quoad nos* in his dynamic interrelatedness to us in all the many aspects of that interrelation, not in his eternal aseity. This unavoidable character of modern theology, as growing out of and confined to the range of our own total experience, means that theological understanding is set in terms of our dynamic, changing, and interrelated experience. The divine ultimacy that we name is an ultimacy in intrinsic relation to our contingency, relativity, and transience. The divine intentionality or will that we can trust is one directive of the dynamic course of our life and history. The divine favor or grace that we can proclaim is manifested in the relation of God's Word to our finite and wayward condition. God, if he exists at all for us, is thus dynamic, related, and changing; he is in process, if he is to be ground, ruler, and redeemer of *our* process. This dynamic, active, related character of modern theological language —required by the cognitive limits of modern experience and our modern sense of the reality and value of the contingent creaturely world to which God is related—is the reason the biblical rather than the Greek view of God has been and continues to be so congenial to theologians both Protestant and Catholic in our time.[1] It also implies a new dialectical relation between understanding through stories and understanding through analysis, between mythical speech and philosophical language.

If the fundamental form of theological language is that of philosophical analysis—analysis of the permanent and necessary (ontological) structures of present experience —then the resulting view of God is either too immanent or too transcendent to fit the realities of Christian experience or the clear implications of basic Christian symbols. In Christian symbol and experience God represents an ultimacy that is related to our changeability, a transcendence that is the ground of our transience, an absoluteness that is in relation to our relativity. Now if God is conceived exhaustively and determinatively in the terms of our contingent, relative, transient, and autonomous experience, then he is understood as univocally illustrative of the same categories as structure our being, and so as a part of, wholly immanent in, the structure of process, a being among the beings of the world.[2] To be sure, God can be conceived as dynamic, related, changing, and intentional; yet, since in this conception God has too little transcendence and no real ultimacy, the concept confines and warps rather than expresses the deepest meanings inherent in Christian symbols and experience. Correspondingly, if through a structural, philosophical analysis God's transcendence and ultimacy are expressed, and thus the ontological categories of our finitude are essentially negated rather than univocally affirmed vis-à-vis God, as in classical theism; then God's dynamic, related, changing character is fatally compromised. The philosophical notion of God then contradicts the divine relatedness and activity implied in Christian symbolism and experience, and the God spoken of ceases to be the God named in and through our dynamic and transient experience.

I am suggesting that modernity has inescapably related God and our talk about God to experience, that as a consequence any meaningful and valid concept of God must be set in dynamic, active, related terms. And, finally, if in this situation the divine ultimacy and transcendence, in its paradoxical relation to our changing life, is to be expressed, story language, the symbolic language of "myth," the dynamic language of activity, creative work, guiding and ruling, as well as the language of intentional promises and purposes, must be used. The fundamental symbols expressive of the universal activity of God in creation and in providence are thus symbols expressible only in dynamic, active, related, and intentional forms of speech, the language appropriate for purposive actors in a dramatic story.

In sum, the strange relation of God's transcendence and ultimacy to the immanence of our general experience requires for the theology a peculiar mode of "story" or mythical language.[3] Modern theology in a scientific and philosophical world is just as bound to "mythical" discourse, to a symbolic language that has a story form, as in the prereflective world of the earliest strata of the Old Testament.

2. It is characteristic of our community's tradition and faith that while God is thus dynamically related to all experience, he is nevertheless known most clearly and decisively in certain places and through certain events and persons—in a certain definite, restricted, and infinitely particular segment of nature and of history. Thus it is to the covenant history with Israel and to the person of Jesus that theological understanding looks for its principle and determinative naming of God. In turn, this basic structure characteristic of Christian faith, and its reflective understanding that is theology, contains three important implications for our problem:

Theological understanding includes as an essential aspect of its task telling, comprehending, and interpreting a number of historical stories, such as the story of Jesus. To be sure, the story that is here told, whatever its doctrinal or conceptual form, involves more than mere historical narrative, since in its traditional forms it expresses within that history the unique activity of the divine that is the ground and goal of all history. But since Christianity is founded on historical events, we can never cease to tell historical stories (or elaborate historical promises) in Christian theology; these stories do not derive from analysis of present experience and cannot be expressed in its terms in any exhaustive way.

This essential relation of Christian theology to a particular history inevitably implies that God acts differently or uniquely in certain times and places, that certain events and sections of history are for us more revelatory than others of the depths of his divine being and the mystery of his divine purposes. Thus for any Christian theology there are *uniquely* unique events,[4] qualitatively different from other events, and thus by implication ontologically different, in relation to the divine activity. Thus mythical language about God is again inevitable—in this case language about his special deeds in history, his mighty works —however we may in the elaboration of our theology understand and philosophically conceptualize that religious language. The central Christian symbols expressive of the "special activity" of God in revelation and in redemption thus in another way imply a dramatic language of story and, insofar as *God* is here at work, a language analogous to the older language of "myth." Understanding through philosophical analysis can only uncover the general, pervasive, and universal structures of actuality—what cannot fail to be there and so what is always there.[5] These ontological and metaphysical structures are vastly important for theological elaboration. However, a Christian (or Jewish) theology must also speak of God's special deeds and special relations, and so of special past and future histories, and that means a story about God's work in the past or in the future, different from the dynamic omnipresent and continuous aspects of the divine activity, however particular and novel the results of that latter activity may be in nature and history generally. Theological language therefore involves not only dynamic language about God's general activity, and historical language about certain events, but also entails mythical language about God's special role in those crucial events through which we know the character, intention, and goal of his general activity.

The historical character of Christian faith implies that the most important understanding for us to have about God—the depths of his being and his purposes—is found only in relation to those special events. An analysis of nature and its course, of history and its turbulences, of man's being and its ambiguity, may reveal much about the ultimacy known to us, but such general, speculative knowledge of deity cannot be taken as the conceptual *clue*, the guiding model, lest the divine be made either too immanent or too transcendent. If special historical events are uniquely revelatory of God, then analyses of general experience are not sufficient for a Christian theological understanding of God. Mystery and ambiguity at the most fundamental levels remain when we look at nature, history and ourselves. Only in the event of Jesus as the Christ is clarity with regard to ultimacy manifest. Such an affirmation of meaning despite the mystery of general experience also calls for a special mode of language. Analysis, scientific or philosophical, cannot answer our most fundamental questions; the knowable structure of our experienced world leaves us with an ambiguity. Thus, if meaning is to be affirmed *within* that essential ambiguity, if hope is to be grounded despite that all encompassing mystery, then some form of language beyond that of analysis is necessary, and we return to the language of story, of special histories, and their unique relation to the activity of God.

The paradoxical relation in Christianity between concrete historical events and the transcendent mystery of the divine being and will requires a language that points beyond present structures of depth and mystery to transcendence and the future, and to special events and "deeds." To talk of special concrete events or acts as expressive of a divine being and a divine intention otherwise unknown requires a symbolic speech similar to the language of myth. Myth is the historical language of action used to express a relation to an ultimacy that transcends history and all action. Again, I do not see how modern theology can dispense with some form of this language as long as Christian faith finds itself pointing to a particular history in order to talk significantly about what transcends, guides, and fulfills all history.

3. Finally, a Christian understanding of God is *intentional* in form. Our relation to him concerns the deepest levels of our own personal being, our moral willing, and our purposes. To understand his relation to us requires those categories with which we understand this level of ourselves, namely, those referred to as "spiritual." In describing ourselves we speak of self-awareness, intelligence, will, and purpose. How these are to be understood in relation to the divine being as a whole is a complex theological and philosophical matter. But that God is spirit as well as being and life, that he is the principle of truth and goodness as well as of existence, and that there is in this sense an analogy between the fullness of his being and ours is usually assumed in Christian theology.

God, we affirm, is the source of our being and our life. Our reception of these gifts from him does not depend on our intentionality; in receiving our life from the world and ultimately from him, we do not need either to experience him, be aware of him, or believe in him, that is, to have a "personal" relation to him. Nor do we need to know and believe in order for God to rule our history, however he may do that. On the other hand, despite these important aspects of the divine activity (expressed in the symbols of creation and providence) that relate us to God but not necessarily through our *personal* being, the center of the Christian relation to God is still "intentional" in character. It is an aspect of our self-awareness, of our conscious, personal life, participated in by our cognitive and volitional faculties, and determined ultimately by our inner freedom, a "centered" relation in which our personal assent, acknowledgement, commitment, and decision are effective and dominant. This personal relation to God involves, therefore, not only a knowledge of God's being—

that he is and that he is the source and sovereign over our existence—but also an awareness of the divine as *meaning*, as answering questions that the moral and intentional dimensions of our own existence raise about good and evil in ourselves and in history, and about the ends and purposes of our life and of history generally. Thus Christian theology speaks of the divine intentions or will; it characterizes God as righteous and the "judge" of ourselves and the world; and it knows God as love and forgiveness and therefore as "redeemer" of ourselves and our world. The category of the divine being in relation to our contingent being is all important. But it is important for us as personal beings, who live in a dimension of meaning as well, because that divine being is also qualified by love; and the knowledge of the divine being is redemptive for us inwardly only if we can respond to that divine being, so known, in a personal trust and hope that are based on this understanding of God as love.

The center of the Christian relation to God, then, as the Reformers rightly argued, is not onotological but personal in character. Faith is not primarily an assent to speculative truth about the ultimate character of being or about the inhabitants of the universe, divine or creaturely; it is rather at its center a personal response to the intentional presence of God as judgment, love, and the promise of fulfillment. Thus the most fundamental relation of God to man and of man to God in our religion is one of dramatic encounter, of a relation or communion of persons, not one of impersonal forces. God is spirit, and they that worship him must do so in spirit and in truth.

Alfred North Whitehead has elegantly argued that understanding through philosophical analysis can lead to a concept of God in which the divine intentionality relates to our personal freedom. Actuality for Whitehead is essentially an *inward* event, a purposive self-realization in relation to the given and the divine purposes. And Whitehead's philosophical analysis in this connection, as in the specification of dynamic categories for understanding God's relation to the whole cosmos, can be of great help in Christian theology. Nevertheless, such an understanding of actuality as universally intentional is a rationalized form of myth. An ontology of free and purposive events makes ontology itself an understanding through a succession of stories, of personal histories. But more: if the divine intentionality is transcendent to the structure of events, and thus the sovereign lord of them, and able to break into that structure with a *new* creation, a *new* message, and a *new* hope; if the divine activity works in the world with varying actions according to new situations; if history is thus genuinely dramatic, a new compound of God's *novum* and our creativity; then only dramatic language in theology, the language of personal and historical action, can express the Christian view of history and of God's creative part in it. Again, a modern theology concerned about issues of sin and salvation, and therefore about personal and social history, and about the future and our confidence in it, must use the language of story, personal action, and promise, as well as the language of ontological analysis, when it speaks of God.

Despite the rise to dominance in our cultural life first of metaphysical analysis and subsequently of scientific analysis, modern Christian theology must retain, refine, and revitalize the traditional language of mythic symbols. Such a mode of speech includes language about God in the form of his historical activity, and therefore recitation of crucial events; and it also involves language about God that includes the dimension of spirit and meaning, and that centers its affirmations around the divine intentionality, the divine will, and the divine purposes. Every fundamental Christian symbol—creation, providence, revelation, incarnation, atonement, justification, sanctification, and the eschatological promises—has at its heart this intentional character; it specifies the meaning and the purpose of each phase of the divine activity and thus of the divine will and intention as central to what the Christian knows and affirms about God. In this sense, since the symbols of our religion retain, convey, and perpetuate mythical elements into Christian theological speech, no theological elaboration of these symbols, however philosophical in character, can shed these modes of speech and remain Christian. Personal discourse about God, however we understand its application to the divine nature, is thus intrinsically a part of Christian theology.

This argument might seem to be a studied defense of Reformation and neo-Reformation modes of Protestant theology, of what has been called "biblical theology"—where language about God is basically comprised of a recitation of God's "mighty acts" in history, a language derived directly and without philosophical mediation from the forms and categories of the biblical witness. Here, as in the Bible itself, God is pictured in personal and historical categories alone, as an unconditioned or absolute personal agent, knowing, intending, and willing his world and certain events in it, dynamically and purposely at work in time and history, and the sovereign Lord, judging, redeeming, and guiding his people and his world to their fulfillment.[6] As is well known, this type of theology, both in the Reformation and in its contemporary neo-Reformation forms, in various ways repudiated or sought to repudiate almost all types of understanding by analysis, whether philosophical or scientific, as intrinsic to theology. I have elsewhere rejected this view of theology as inaccurate and insufficient, though clearly there is much validity in it. Let us now see why this rejection is important, in relation first to science and then to philosophy, and so why understanding by analysis is *also* an essential part of theological understanding.

First of all, science has in the last two hundred years changed what we mean in theology by "understanding through stories." Science was largely instrumental in developing in its modern form the concept of "religious symbol," which is central to the present Christian theological enterprise. As was noted, early myths, and all early Christian theology, told stories about God's acts in history that included certain spatio-temporal facts. For example, the story (or symbol) of creation thus included, at least implicitly, *knowledge* of how old the world was, how the rocks, seas, mountains, trees, animals, and man came to be, who the first pair were, where they lived, and what they did, and so on. And the same inclusion of "factual" components as well as "transcending" components characterized other fundamental symbols, for example, providence, incarnation, revelation, and eschatology. Modern sciences—geology, astronomy, biology, and history—have taken as *their* preserve these *factual* elements of traditional theological stories (of what we are calling the symbols). The more these sciences discovered about the universe and its history, the more factual errors in the accounts of Scripture and of tradition they seemed to uncover. Today theologians can no longer assert a fact merely on the basis of a theological story or symbol, whether related to the symbol of creation, the fall, providence, incarnation, or eschatology. We go to anthropology, not to dogmatics, to find out what the earliest men and women were probably like, where they lived, and what they did. It is, to be sure, essential for Christology that certain historical events, like the birth, life, and death of Jesus, occurred. But only historical inquiry itself can assure us of these "facts," or tell us what sort of events they were—just as astrophysics, geology, biology, and anthropology, not the hypotheses of a theological faculty, can tell us about the beginnings of earth, the origins of life, and the early history of mankind. The canon of the

autonomy of human understanding, and thus the integrity
of the sciences, which we all accept in our daily life and
therefore must accept in principle in theology as well,
requires us to admit that a dogmatic statement, a doctrine, even a sacred "story of the incarnation," cannot assure us of any of the *factual* elements ingredient to the
doctrine. To deny this is to deny our own integrity as
assenting members of a modernity that trusts in science
and autonomy, an assent in ourselves that is undeniably
apparent every time we go to a doctor or fly in an air-
plane. This assent to a "morality of truth" involved in all
scientific inquiry is the source of the greatest tensions between biblical scholarship, based on that inquiry, and
dogmatic theology[7] (as it is also the source of the tension
between the historical study of Christian doctrine and the
theological affirmation of a dogma). No dogmatic statement can establish or guarantee the truth of a historical
fact, even a fact essential to the meaning and validity of
the dogmatic assertion in question.

Through this development in the relationship between
scientific inquiry and theology, the character or form of
the mythical or "story" language inherent in fundamental
Christian symbols has changed. What has appeared is a
"symbol" in a new sense that now excludes the older or
literal "story" form. The symbol of creation now contains
no information about the age of the earth or the early
forms of its life; the symbol of the fall no longer includes
the "story" of a literal Adam and Eve and their activities.
Creation and fall have become essentially and exclusively
*symbols* respectively expressive of the basic relation of
God to his world, and of the human condition in relation
to God, self, and others. No longer are they bearers of
factual statements, available to scientific or historical inquiry and testing, about past occurrences. One of the
most important achievements of recent Protestant and
Catholic theology, making possible its acclimatization to

that modern view of truth that we all accept, has been this slow, and still in many quarters controversial, development of the modern view of a theological symbol, different from every previous view.

A religious symbol here is a notion which, as Paul Ricoeur has said, invites conceptuality and factual content, but does not itself contain them. It does not in itself entail or assert, though it may refer to, any factual propositions. Nor is it a clearly defined concept in a philosophical system. It is thus the *basis* of doctrinal and dogmatic formulation, that which the doctrines and dogmas of the past, and the theological elaborations of the present, seek to express conceptually. What it does for each generation is to shape in a *Christian* way that ultimate horizon in which all our concepts make sense, and to provide the general framework within which we interpret all facts. Religious symbols, and any system of such symbols, form that "world" within which we understand nature, ourselves, others, history, and our common destiny. Creation, fall, providence, revelation, incarnation and atonement, *ecclesia*, Word, sacrament, and eschatology: these are symbols that together express a Christian horizon of lived experience, for each expresses the relation, apprehended in faith, of God to the various facets and dimensions of our total experience. These Christian symbols do not tell us facts; rather, they set all the facts we know, by inquiry, experience, or anticipation, into a Christian form. Christian symbols give a Christian interpretation of our world; they shape our reflective experience of our being in the world by providing a Christian form to the horizon of ultimacy. All understanding by analysis, philosophical or scientific, requires such symbolic foundations, and every science indirectly and every philosophy directly illustrates this dependence. Christian symbols express the way in which ultimacy forms and manifests itself for us as Christians; they name the totality and the mystery in which we exist. Such symbols, now no longer in themselves simple stories though they may refer to stories, nevertheless retain a "story" form: they tell us of divine intentions, actions, and deeds. And thus dynamically and intentionally relating transcendence and ultimacy to our changing world, they speak to us of the Christian God.

If fundamental theological notions are thus "symbols," forms in terms of which experience is to be thematized, then clearly they are, not unlike Kant's categories, "empty" unless they receive content from our experience. Part of their meaning comes from their own unique *Christian* shape, what we will call their "eidetic" meaning. But part of their meaning, and therefore their power over us and our sense of their validity, comes from the experience that they thematize: experience of ourselves, our world, history, and experience of the divine ultimacy that grounds and pervades that experience.

Thus religious symbols inevitably change and develop in their meanings as man's cultural experience and forms of reflections on that experience change. The experience they shape into Christian forms shifts itself as history and culture shift, as man's self-interpretation and his interpretation of his world change. Because of the new visions of the cosmos and its processes of development that modern science has given us, the symbol of creation has a different meaning for us than it did for Tertullian or Augustine, Thomas or Calvin; our understanding of the world we affirm to be divinely created has changed, and so our understanding of that symbol has changed. If that meaning has *not* changed, if *creatio ex nihilo* or the symbol of incarnation as dogmas have a *changeless* meaning, then they have no real meaning for us as thematizations of our world and our history and of God's relation to them. They are empty forms devoid of live content, a situation common in the church. Dogmas are conceptual interpretations of more fundamental symbols, interpretations, or

doctrinal formulations agreed upon by the church in one
age and so set in the conceptual forms of that time. Inevitably, therefore, they become subject to historical development, and ultimately their conceptual categories
become anachronistic to a later age, needing critical evaluation and fundamental reinterpretation and reconception. In a basic sense, symbols, and not dogmas, develop
and change; for each dogma, like every doctrinal formulation in theology, is the historical formulation at a given
moment of the church's understanding of the basic symbols essential to her life. Symbols become reflective concepts and, in the Catholic tradition, dogmas, thought out
and thought about, in terms of the self-understanding and
the understanding of the world of their time.

This understanding of religious symbols, calling for interpretive theory rather than providing such theory,
means in turn that understanding by analysis, both scientific and philosophical, contributes positively to the
theological meaning for us of these symbols. We cannot
legitimately and meaningfully conceive except in terms of
the world *we* inhabit. Our concepts of ultimacy, our theological notions, have meaning for us only if they thematize and shape our experience and our world. If they do
not, they are transcendent and changeless, empty and lifeless. The implications of this for our experience of ourselves, our world, and our destiny will be the subject of
the next chapter. Now I wish to conclude by giving the
implications of this view of symbols for our reflection, for
our conceptual and theological understanding of the symbols of our faith.

If, for example, we are to conceive theologically the
work of God as the source of finite being (creation), and
the work of God in history (providence), we must conceive these symbols, which give Christian shape to our
reflections, in terms of *our* understanding of our world
and our history. This involves on the first level the under-

standing that scientific analysis provides: the natural, the
social, and the historical sciences. For these form *our*
world; we believe in them, and we cannot conceive that
world in opposition to their major implications. For we
live in the world of modernity, and we believe in their
account of it! But more fundamentally, this modern world
that we inhabit, in large part created by scientific inquiry
and in which God works, is structured for us in terms of
modern ontology. Such ontologies express most directly
the way reflectively we are in the world. We do experience space, time, substance, and causality in modern
modes; we experience inwardness, freedom, and autonomy in modern modes. In turn, modern ontologies give
reflective form to this modern being in the world and the
modern experiencing of that being. No theological interpretation of fundamental symbols can have meaning for
us, therefore, unless it gives Christian shape to some *modern* ontology, expressive of our own being in the world. In
providing understanding of the symbols expressive of our
faith, theology for its own completion calls for the appropriation and use of contemporary philosophy if the symbols it expresses are to be reflectively alive, that is, meaningful and valid for us.

Thus symbol becomes concept—a doctrine, an object
of reflection—by shaping our being in the modern world
reflected in science and ontology. In turn what we understand by analysis—all we know by science expressed in
general structures through ontological analysis—provides
the filling, the materials, and contents, to the theological
symbols. The symbols call then for a relation to ordinary,
modern experience if they are to be alive in our existence;
and they call for modern ontological explications if they
are to be *thought*, if they are to be genuine modes of our
own deepest reflection. Understanding by stories and understanding by analysis, therefore, complement and determine each other. Our most fundamental language about

God, originating in the forms of historical and mythical stories, now embodied in fundamental symbols, provides the ultimate shape in terms of which we reflectively conceive modern experience and our modern world. In turn, all we know by analysis of ourselves and our world provides living content for our Christian naming of the ultimacy upon which we depend.

# Chapter IV

## Sources and Tradition

TO EXPLICATE the use of sources and tradition in theological understanding I would like to suggest another dialectic, different from the previous one between understanding through stories and understanding through analysis. The relevant dialectic in this case is between traditional symbols and present experience—knowledge, understanding, and appropriation of sources in the past and our lived experience today.

Tradition makes the modern man uneasy, even the middle-aged man if it is his father's tradition. The natural direction of our modern gaze is toward the present and the future, and our wish is to look at both present and future with what we call "open eyes," unimpeded by the blinders of the prejudices and dogmas of the past. In fact for us tradition as a word, and even the past as a source and ground of relevant wisdom, seems almost equivalent to prejudice, stultifying conservatism, or even the defense of vested interests.[1]

Now there is no doubt that such wary skepticism about tradition, its dogmas, and vested interests, has valid historical grounds. Protestants first felt to their discomfort this heavy stifling hand of their own tradition a hundred and fifty or more years ago and have been conscious of it

ever since. And many a present Catholic, looking ner-
vously over his shoulder at sounds emanating from Rome,
knows this negative reaction to "tradition" very well. An
absolutized tradition, and its modes of thinking, believing,
worshipping, and acting, can be a danger to creative
thinking and living alike. As the eighteenth century (tradition!) has taught us, tradition can *only* be positive when
it is balanced dialectically by the needs of the present and
the future; when it is precisely *not* an absolute authority
but on the contrary when it has undergone some relativi-
zation in relation to present and future. They alone can
genuinely love, inwardly appropriate, and creatively use
tradition who are in part free of it, who experience a creative autonomy over against its demands, and who are capable of reworking tradition in the light of the needs and
possibilities of the present and future.

Even in this modern wisdom, however, there can be an
optical illusion, symbolized by our reference to the eighteenth-century *tradition*. For the "open eyes" of modernity, unimpeded by traditional dogmas and assenting only
to hypotheses generated by present analysis and testable
in future experience, are not themselves merely "natural,"
as if in this open empiricism all traditional elements had
been stripped away and only the "bare" and "natural"
mind were at work. Rather, in fact, the anti-traditional
bias of modernity is itself a potent tradition, and one of
long standing. It is a way of viewing experience and our
reflections upon it that is itself a cultural, historical product, an empirical attitude toward truth and value that has
been slowly generated out of an impressive scientific,
philosophical, literary, moral, and political inheritance
stretching back through the nineteenth century, the Enlightenment, and at least to the Renaissance and the Reformation, and behind them to the Roman and the Hellenic worlds. Moreover, this tradition was enshrined in
and communicated through important "symbols" concern-

ing nature and reason, man and his powers of knowing and doing, "facts" and their relation to theory, and the nature of truth and the way to find it. And like all traditions, this empirical and scientific tradition was embodied in important communities—scientific, academic, and social—and its symbols, standards, and goals were passed on from master scientist or academic to apprentice through the arts of communication and of educational formation.

As even this brief analysis of the historical background of possibly the most "anti-traditional" of forms of thought reveals, all human thinking takes place within a cultural tradition and in large measure is based on a cultural tradition. We see, even when we look solely at the present and the future, with eyes formed by the past; and all our reflection on what we see is structured by the language and the categories we have absorbed from our tradition, and that we use to criticize it. Thus even our most radically open investigations are already "theory-laden." For the questions we ask, the data we think important, the categories of explanation we consider relevant, the standards we employ for assent, and the goals of our inquiry are set for us by the tradition and the community in which we live and think.

This is not to deny that there are creative moments in cultural and religious history when radically new visions appear that transform or even overturn much of what had been experienced and thought before. These occur in science, philosophy, politics, and the arts. But these "revolutionary" events are as rare in cultural life as they are in religion. And as every historical account of a new creation evidences, the possiblity of these "revolutionary moments" is dependent upon the social and cultural conditions that preceded them and thus set their stage, and upon certain traditional ways of regarding things, a history of symbols, standards and goals, which are in that moment appropriated and used in a new way and so result in a new vision. No political or economic revolution is possible or fruitful unless it arises out of both a history of widespread social dislocation and a developing "self-consciousness" on the part of advancing social forces that in turn have a long history in philosophy, religion, and social ideas. And cultural "revolutions," whether in science, philosophy, or religion, also have a preceding history of ideas, values, and attitudes that set the stage for a new synthesis; as the present crisis in Catholicism amply illustrates, born as it is out of modernity in relation to changing views of religious authority, truth, and value. Tradition is thus a necessary base even of new social and cultural structures, since nothing human arises totally *de novo* out of its historical matrix. But, as is evident from these examples, tradition can be the *source* of new creativity only when it is in part relativized. An absolutized tradition can only resist historical change; it cannot creatively absorb and deal with it. Thus it seeks to move above the changing forms of thought and life, and so in the process of historical becoming, it slowly divests itself of meaning, relevance, and creative vitality. It is ripe, then, for historical extinction. Only if the symbols embodied in a tradition are continually *reinterpreted* is a tradition alive and well in historical process; and only if the community that bears the tradition is open for new structures, can that community, and its tradition, retain its creativity and strength. Modern science has built this sense of dynamic change into its own most essential notions of inquiry and truth; modern political and religious systems (though in all their forms —democratic, Marxist, Catholic, or Protestant—they were founded on "revolutionary moments" of the past) have by no means followed suit.

Whenever in turn such visions in religion, philosophy, science, politics, morals, and art, occurring at revolutionary moments or *Kairoi* in historical time, become cultur-

ally formative and thus historically important, and the
mode of thought and existence of a community, they become a "tradition" forming the life and thought of those
who exist within that cultural community. Thus it is that
all human products are historically relative, to the time
and place, the community, its language and its ethos,
within which the human creation appears. In this sense,
religious or cultural tradition always has two main facets
or elements: it is embodied in a community, bound together by a common ethos, standards, and goals—
whether it is a political, religious, or scientific community.
And the community exists spiritually in and through its
symbols, which express its shared view of its world,
of man and his powers, of value, truth, and the standards
relevant to each, and of destiny, the fulfillment of men
and women. When, therefore, people become aware of
their tradition as a threat or a hindrance to their autonomy and creativity, instead of as a resource for both, they
do so because in fact they have partially entered *another*
tradition. The sudden awareness in many Catholics during the last decade of their own tradition as *heteronomous*, external, "extrinsic," and stifling to creative thought,
belief, and life—the deepest cause of the present crisis—
is primarily due to their possibly unconscious entrance
into the secular community of modernity, a "tradition"
with symbolic thematizations of reality, truth, and value
vastly different from those of traditional Catholicism.

Modernity with its ideals of autonomy, freedom, and
"openness for the future" has, therefore, not at all dis-
pensed with the need for tradition,[2] community, and symbols if we are to think, act, and exist creatively. What is
new, or at least different, from what we easily call "traditional cultures," is a recognition of the need for autonomous, present, and creative *appropriation* of any given
tradition if it is to be a living tradition, and of the plurality of our spiritual communities—and thus the possible

choice each of us has to make of the fundamental symbols and of the community within which we are to exist spiritually. None of us any longer are "born" Catholics, Protestants, or even Christians or Jews; we are not even any longer born "modern" if the counterculture continues as a pervasive option! We have in some measure to choose, to give inward and free assent to a community and tradition, if we are to live within it—a point always emphasized in the theory and the rites of both Catholicism and Protestantism but now made actual for all of us by the pluralism of modernity. We have, then, to choose as modern men and women, and thus our present is relatively free of our past. But what we have to choose is a community and a way of looking at things, a set of symbols, embodied in that community. There is no escape from tradition. Even the most radically empirical of scientists joins the community of science, addresses it in his creative work, submits his conclusions and career to its standards and judgments, and consents in his work to the symbols of empiricism and the norms of integrity historically determinative of that community. And even the most radically rebellious of Catholics (or Protestants of seventy-five years ago), impatient with every facet of the tradition that nourished them, feel and think that way about their tradition because they have first unconsciously and then consciously joined the community of modernity with its traditions of empiricism, relativism, autonomy, and naturalism.

We are, then, back in the arms of tradition, symbols, and community. We are inescapably *historical* creatures, formed by our past, and we face present life in its terms. Of course this truth that all truth emanates from a tradition, its community, and its symbols, has given shape to much conservative and neoconservative modern theology, both Catholic and Protestant. We exist, says this viewpoint, in the biblical (or the Catholic) tradition, and therefore our theological reflection is to be formed solely from that tradition and in terms of its symbols alone— biblical in its Protestant forms, dogmatic, metaphysical and Thomistic in its Catholic ones. And we are called to proclaim this tradition to the unbelieving world with its secularistic, humanistic tradition.

There is also an optical illusion in this viewpoint: it is the illusion that we can exist spiritually in a religious tradition and historically or actually in the quite different tradition of modernity, and keep the two quite separate. Namely, that we can drive cars, fly in planes, and go to doctors, and not *believe* in some important measure in the modern world of science and naturalistic philosophy; and that we can act politically and live as humans in our communities, and not *believe* the modern anthropologies of autonomy and the modern philosophies of society, history, and temporal passage. This is to forget what we have just told modernity in our defense of theological understanding, namely, that to live creatively is precisely to live in community, and to live in community is to accept as our own its basic symbols, standards, and goals—and from there to think all that we think. Thus a Catholicism, or a Protestantism, whose people (clerical or lay) are immersed spiritually as well as bodily in the modern world, must reinterpret its religious heritage in the terms of that world if that heritage is to be alive for them. A religious tradition quite unrelated to the world in which its people seek to exist is not a *tradition*: it is an anachronism, at best a museum, at worst a mortuary.

The fact is that the people in the churches do live, one hopes, in two communities. I say "one hopes" because our actual existence—where we live, work, play, act, and think—is the community of modernity, a radically secular community suffused with a naturalistic ontology and a this-worldly scheme of values. This is the community of our daily life, our *Lebenswelt*, if not the community of our reading. And thus it is *this* community that forms us, and gives to us our fundamental sense of what is real, true, and of value. To live and participate in that community, inwardly and outwardly as we all do, is to live in and from its own most fundamental symbols, and thus to be in large part ourselves secular and naturalistic. It is therefore difficult for any of us to live in the world of another tradition, even an inherited and revered religious tradition, since we are now suffused in the living tradition of modernity. The most fundamental theological problems for us all—Christians, Jews, Buddhists—arise precisely here: we exist in modernity and among its symbols; we understand ourselves, others, and our world largely (even if unconsciously) in its terms. Thus its effect on our participation in that other tradition, our inherited religious tradition, is overwhelming, whether we practice exegesis, hermeneutics, or theology professionally, or just try to be a Christian. As I have noted, this interaction between a powerful modernity where most Catholics now live spiritually, as well as physically, has been the major cause of the crisis, turmoil, and threatened disintegration of traditional Catholic thought and life.

The reason for this intense difficulty for theology and for belief in the midst of modernity is twofold. Since the community of our daily life is *the* formative community, formative of our most basic sense of reality, truth, and value, it is difficult for another fundamental viewpoint, represented by other symbolic expressions, to be meaningful or deeply valid to us. We can, to be sure, assent to traditional Catholic or Protestant symbols; but it is hard for us to know what they *mean* unless they become in some real measure part of the modern world where we live, unless some conceptual, existential, and ethical mediation or union is achieved between the two traditions in which we try to live. Is this part of the reason so many

able Catholic philosophers insist on a sharp division between philosophy and theology, the former representing
the tradition of modernity where they *really* live, and the
latter the religious tradition where they wish or feel they
*ought* to live? And they keep them radically separate because they have no intelligible way of mediating them by
thought, because only in terms of separation can both
continue together to be held.

More basically, the reason for the difficulty of theology
in our day is that a symbol—religious, philosophical, or
political—is creative for us only when it shapes or forms
our actual, lived experience. Without that content given it
by lived experience, a symbol, however profound it may
be or however vigorous our conscious assent, is not functioning; it has no role, and so it floats above our life as an
empty notion, adored but inert; and life continues on
other terms and for other gods. As I have argued elsewhere,[3] the tragedy of modern culture is that its traditional, and most fundamental, religious symbols are out of
touch with modern experience; and thus they are empty
and lifeless. And on the other hand, modern experience,
too secular to take symbols of ultimacy seriously, is itself
given no creative shape or unity with regard to our ultimate origins and destiny, our deepest fears and our most
crucial hopes.

There are two more implications for theological understanding of this theme to be noted before we proceed:
first, the apologetic task (relating traditional theological
symbols to the common ground of modern experience,
sensibilities, and concepts) is not a task relevant merely
in relation to the unbelieving world outside the church.
For as the crisis within Catholicism shows, the church
lives in that world of modernity and, for good or ill, believes in that world. Thus apologetics is a task essential to
*church* theology, to the theologian talking to himself as a
modern man as well as to others, and to the church speak-

ing to herself in confessing her faith—lest what is said in either case mean nothing. The principle reason the Curia may not see this point is that the world of modernity in which we live here and in northern Europe has not yet penetrated spiritually very far south of Milan, though with *autostrada* and Fiats, it will soon enough!

Second, the deepest problem that interaction with modernity raises for present Catholicism is not what is called the "development of dogma," the historical and changing character of fundamental doctrine. This assumes the illusion of two "given" and thoroughly substantial communities, one secular and one religious, which interpenetrate only enough to force the symbols of the one to take the reflective forms of the other. The present problem is *not* that for the modern mind the changeless forms of dogma must change, and how theologically we are to understand the historicity in which we are inescapably immersed, that is, the problem of the *historical* consciousness of modernity that we share. The problem is that in the modernity in which we live it is difficult, if not impossible, to be theological at all, to find any meaningful form to fundamental doctrine, much less a changeless form. Our problem is not of a *changing* theology but of any theology at all, the problem of the *secular* consciousness of modernity that we also share. Until Catholicism has recovered enough from the recent shock of historicism and of losing Chalcedon, Thomism, and natural law as the changeless forms of its reflective and ethical life to recognize this deeper crisis of the possibility in a secular world of any Christology, philosophical theology, or Christian ethics *at all*, it has not tasted the real gall of modernity. Clearly the heart of this problem is that, while none of us like the theologically bitter aftertaste, we *do* like the heady brew of modernity, and we gulp it down more and more without the slightest intention of stopping!

Understanding is made up of tradition and of present

experience, of symbols from our past borne by our community and shaping the present world of lived experience. In this interaction the symbols give that world of experience ultimate coherence, order, illumination, and healing; in turn, experience in its contemporary forms provides the symbols with relevance, reality, and validity. Without such symbols of ultimacy, experience is blind, its joys unexpressed and uncelebrated, its confidences and hopes ungrounded, and its fears unnamed and unconquered. Without the contemporary content of lived experience, traditional symbols are empty, inert, functionless, and marked for death. There is without doubt a latent trinitarian structure here, a trinity of ultimacy, symbol, and present experience; but that is not my present concern.

What, then, does this dialectic of tradition and symbol with present experience mean for the method of theological understanding? How is a modern theology to proceed? What are its major obligations, if it is to encompass this dialectic and provide modern men and women with Christian meaning to their experience, and with the possibilities of contemporary assent and of creative existence? At this stage of our discussion of method I can delineate three separate tasks for theological understanding, and a fourth in the next chapter. The union of these tasks constitutes the creative effort of systematic or constructive theology.

The first is hermeneutical and historical, the delineation of the intrinsic meaning of the symbols central to the Christian tradition. Christian theology is understanding, reflection on, and comprehension of our human experience, our being in the world, in terms of the symbols of the Christian tradition; much as being a Christian is existing (as opposed to reflecting) in the light and the grace of that tradition. Thus the first task of theology is to be clear about the eidetic, intrinsic meaning of these symbols. I have spoken of the meaning (or better in Heidegger's terms, the "sense") of the symbol in relation to lived experience: that in our lives and experience to which these symbols give shape. Now we refer to something else—to the intrinsic form of the symbol in itself, and the *way* it shapes our understanding of our world and ourselves. For different symbols from different traditions, political, philosophical, or religious, shape the same ranges of experience differently. Each system of symbols points or projects a different world, and a different self and others in that world. The Hindu, the Marxist, and the naturalistic understanding of man and his destiny are *different* understandings, and each is in turn different from a Christian or from a Jewish understanding. These differences are embodied within the respective symbols of these various traditions; and it is this intrinsic character of the symbol, unique to a given tradition, that causes the illumination and the healing found in any particular point of view. A Christian understanding of existence is responsible for uncovering and for expressing this eidetic meaning of its own traditional symbols; thus it must begin by an inquiry into those meanings.

Clearly the biblical sources are primary in this investigation as the closest and most significant witnesses to the divine activity foundational to the community and the tradition, an initiating activity expressed originally through this symbolic witness and in the terms of these symbolic interpretations. Each one of these original symbols has a variety of meanings in the whole scripture, and thus they are as plural and relative, as "historical," as anything else among the data of theology. Among the most significant of these symbols for Christian theology are the following: creation, sin or rebellion, God's mighty works or deeds, election, covenant and law, people, promise and fulfillment; divine speech, divine warning, and divine judgment, divine fatherly care, love, mercy, and forgiveness, the divine promise of the new; Son of Man, Son of

God, Logos, Spirit, atoning death, resurrection, new Israel, *eclesia*, final return or *parousia*, and Kingdom.

These symbols are the most fundamental ingredients of theological understanding. Their meanings, in so far as they can be recovered at all, constitute the *norma non normata* of all subsequent Christian witness in teaching and Christian reflective speech. It is evident that none of these individual symbols—and this is true of every religion, philosophy, or political tradition—can be understood alone or in isolation. Rather, each of them receives and maintains its intrinsic meaning in and through the whole cluster or system of symbols in which it functions. Each has "internal relations" to each of the other symbols, and thus the whole forms in principle a systematic unity of meaning that shapes the character of any particular symbol. Creation has the meaning it does in the Old Testament tradition because of its relations to the symbols of Jahveh, the fall, covenant, law, and eschatological expectation, and in the New Testament tradition because of its relations to incarnation, atonement, new birth, and *parousia*; and so on for each symbol in turn. Beyond the scriptural meanings of the symbols, moreover, their meanings in the tradition of the church are also a relevant and an intrinsic part of the data. For tradition is a whole, with originating elements and subsequent reinterpretations and developments of these elements. And it is through the community's interpretations and reinterpretations of these primary symbols that our own illumination, theological understanding, present interpretation of the original biblical symbols[4] have themselves been shaped. Scripture and tradition are two aspects of one historical source. They are by no means independent of one another, as traditional Protestantism and post-Tridentine Catholicism have both stated; rather in each stage of the way they have interpenetrated one another, and so they must be interpreted together.

This hermeneutical task is *historical,* and in large part a work of objective historical scholarship. In this phase of theological work, the major question is not the existential relevance and truth of these symbols for us, what they might or do mean to *our* existence. Rather the question concerns what the symbols meant for them: for the Hebrews at that period of their history, for Mark, Paul, Augustine, Calvin, or Schleiermacher. We try to see how they saw their being in the world in the light of these symbols, and thus what sort of objective structure that world, self, history, future, and above all, the Lord of that history had for them. Our object is *their* understanding of the symbol, not our own, lest what has possible meaning and validity for us impede or distort our comprehension of what was true for them.

There are, moreover, two other meanings of the word "objective" with regard to this descriptive, historical task in theology. The first has to do with historical inquiry. Many of the crucial symbols of the Christian tradition— revelation, covenant, incarnation, atonement, for example —involve within the orbit of their meanings historical persons, events, and actions. Now although assertion of or belief in the symbol does not for us guarantee or establish the validity of the fact or facts associated with it, still in a *historical* faith (one grounded in events in history and whose symbols concern or interpret those events and their ultimate meaning) stories or histories—in this sense, narrations—form an unavoidable component. Thus historical scholarship into the *historical* realities presupposed by the textual and symbolic witness is likewise unavoidable. As Gerhard Von Rad and Wolfhart Pannenberg have remarked, we can no longer accept as literally true the reports of the scripture concerning the factual character of this history. Therefore, if we are concerned with the theological meaning of that history, knowledge of it through objective inquiry is an inescapable part of theology.[5]

While, then, the *interest* in this history on the part of the theological historian may be a function of his faith, the conclusions of his inquiry into that history cannot themselves be a function of his faith, nor determined by the dogmatic requirements of his tradition. With regard to this history, lying back of the text of the Old Testament, of the New Testament, or of the life of the church, in so far as each can be reconstructed, the most objective historical inquiry is required if theology is to have any legitimacy at all among modern men and women.

Secondly, in this hermeneutical endeavor the object of our inquiry, beside the history lying back of the texts, is the *meaning* of the symbols. This represents an objective meaning in a quite different way. Here we are concerned primarily neither with the subjective intentions, nor the existential situation of the author, nor even the social *Sitz-im-Leben* of the writings themselves, nor with the particular meaning the text had for the readers or its effects on them. These situational and "subjective" elements can be of great importance in understanding the text itself as a historical, literary, and religious document. But for *theological* understanding the main object of inquiry into significant texts is the meaning (or *noema*) of the text, or of the symbol or symbols with which the text is concerned: *the view of self, world, history, the future, and God that the text portrays through the symbols.* This, not the subjectivity of the speaker or the hearer, writer, or reader, is what the text intends to mean: it is its referent, and it forms the primary "meaning" for hermeneutical theology of a biblical or doctrinal symbol. Such a hermeneutical inquiry into a symbol, seeking to explicate its referent, the world it portrays or describes, is an objective inquiry. It requires an empathetic understanding of the world, the horizon, within which this symbol then functioned or had meaning, an empathetic requirement of any historian of ideas with regard to any object of his inquiry. But it re-

quires no faith on our part or assent to any dogmatic belief to achieve its goal. It represents the main intention of
all those historical studies, biblical and doctrinal, con-
nected with theology. Through such inquiry the fundamental symbols of the Christian tradition, in their biblical
and church historical forms, are unconvered, clarified, expressed, and prepared for the work of the theologian.

I have called this hermeneutical task "eidetic," and that
should be explained. The ultimate goal of the inquiry as
far as theology is concerned is a unified, coherent set of
meanings inherent in each major symbol: what "creation"
means, what "providence" entails, what "eschatology" is,
in their past Christian (scriptural and church historical)
forms. Now, as any student of scripture and the history of
doctrine knows well, there is a vast plurality of meanings,
characteristic even of scripture itself, with regard to every
major symbol. These meanings change as history develops
in the Old and New Testaments; and they change as different traditions and writers (such J. and P., Deuteron-
omy, and the prophets; Mark, Paul, and John) used these
symbols. And the variety increases in the history of the
church's interpretations of these same symbols. If the
theologian is to make essential use of this plurality in his
tradition, he must effect (and this is a creative and so
risky task) some unifying synthesis of this diversity of
meanings into one coherent or eidetic meaning. Here the
eidetic meaning of any given symbol expresses that common core of meanings that runs through all the variety of
its traditional and legitimate uses. With the cumulative
development of historical and hermeneutic scholarship
into biblical and doctrinal history, such a synthetic unity
("what the symbol has meant") can hardly be accepted
from the past without criticism or reformulation. It must
be done anew by each generation, and finally by the constructive theologian for himself.

The *symbol*, as an eidetic unity achieved out of a plurality of cases, thus in its role in theology replaces the dogma (or the confessional interpretation of scripture) as the "given" with which the theologian directly works in his own subsequent constructive or systematic task. The creation of this unified symbol is a creative theological task—and so is a risk. Many of the biblical and historical colleagues of the theologian (not to mention the church officials) will probably be horrified. Can any unity out of the diverse meanings of the tradition legitimately be made, his biblical colleagues will ask; must we not live content with this plurality? But each of them must himself assay this task as well if he would use his own scholarly work *theologically*, that is, if he seeks to state the meaning and the truth for the church in his time of these biblical symbols, their relevance for all of us today. No man and no community can live by all forty-four of the Christologies any enthusiastic historical critic can now find in the New Testament.

Thus while the initial aspects of this hermeneutical work are objective, still its final elements are "involved," personal, intuitive, and therefore infinitely risky. Not all symbols can be used, and *a fortiori* not all meanings, biblical or historical, of all symbols. No ready-made meanings of any symbols are given to us unless we retreat and call on a particular historical formulation, a confessional doctrine, or a church dogma to do this interpretive task for us. But to do so would be to ignore this historical task of theology to reinterpret the tradition in the light of all that is now known to be true. To be a "biblical theologian" that is, one who states as best he can the biblical meaning of the major symbols of the biblical tradition, is thus in part a work of constructive theology, an act of creative synthesis. It requires that certain symbols and certain forms of these symbols be taken as central to the entire scripture, to provide the clue for understanding the whole body of biblical materials.

In turn this act of creative synthesis requires that ultimacy does speak to the interpreter through those chosen, central symbols and in those forms. Only in this way is he able to form them for theological use. Amidst all its scholarly tasks, the transition from the study of biblical materials and of the history of doctrine on the one hand to constructive theology on the other requires personal and existential involvement, as well as scholarly objectivity.

The second ingredient of theological understanding calls for an analysis of lived experience: contemporary, ordinary experience. For that is what religious symbols are *about*. They concern the world in which we live and our role in it; they shape the ultimate horizon in which that world exists and moves into the future. Christian symbols give a Christian shape to lived experience if they are to have meaning for us at all. Christian theology is Christian reflection on and Christian understanding of our being in the world. Even if, as in current Catholic eschatological theology, the major Christian symbols talk *about* the future, still they must have meaning *to us* in the present. The past eidetic sense of the symbol is relevant to its Christian shape; but our present human being in the world, as experienced by us, gives actual *meaning* or "sense" to the eidetic meaning. This, following Heidegger, is what we will call the "sense" of the symbol: that aspect of our fundamental experience with which the symbol has to do, which it shapes and fashions into a Christian form. The symbol is empty until it thus shapes our modern experience. We do not know what an eschatological promise *means* until through this symbol *our* experience of our history and future is actively shaped, until that symbol becomes reflectively the way we understand *our* immersion in history and passage into the future. The presupposition here for theological meaning is that modern experience of present and so of future calls for such shaping by religious symbols that it manifests a dimension of ultimacy that must be given a religious and ultimately a Christian form—or else the symbol and the experience can have no possible point of meeting in our present, and the symbol will be forever empty and the experience blind.

Constructive or systematic theology is reflection on the meaning ("sense") and truth of Christian symbols *for us*. Biblical and historical theology are reflection on their meanings for the tradition. If, then, we are to do constructive or systematic theology, we must move from the mere eidetic meaning to that sense in our experience. For if these symbols are not meaningful and true for us, and thus intrinsically related to our experience of ourselves and our world, then there is for us neither religion nor theology. Let us note that here the dogmatic and the apologetic aspects of theology are identical: the meaning of the symbol *is* its meaning for us, the way it coheres, illumines, and heals the experience of self, world, and God. It is probably on this ground as much as any that we each assent to the symbol as true, and seek to declare that validity to others, and it is surely on this ground that we understand what it "means." The meaning of any symbol is radically *experiential*, or there is no meaning for us at all. Thus part of the intrinsic task of theology is an analysis of contemporary, lived experience to uncover those aspects of that experience relevant to each symbol, such as creation, fall, providence, Christology, and eschatology, and then to interpret the symbol as creatively formative of and illuminative in *that* range of contemporary experience. This is the phenomenological and existential side of theology, and it is crucial.

Finally, constructive theology requires for its completion the conceptuality of a modern ontology, given to it by loan from some example of contemporary philosophy. The third ingredient of "meaning" in theological understanding is its ontological meaning, its conceptuality in terms of our most fundamental ways of thinking of the world in which we exist. Theology is a mode of reflection, not merely on our religious or existential experience, our personal being in existential relation to God, though this is surely one major aspect of its meaning. Theology is also *general* reflection: on the nature, conditions, and problems of finite being (as created by God and estranged from him); on the processes of nature and of history (as ruled, judged, and redeemed by God); on the essential character of personhood and community; and on the destiny in the future of nature, self, and history in God. Thus the scope of theology is inclusive of all else that we experience and can think: of space and time, of substance and causality, of terms and relations, of forms and process, of necessity and freedom, of proximate means and ultimate ends. Therefore, what is known in each science is ultimately relevant and related to every essential theological symbol. Every issue of speculative ontology or of philosophy reappears when one seeks to conceive, to think of, a theological symbol in its relation to the totality of our experience. Thus the elaboration of Christian symbols into reflective form, which is theology, requires that each one be conceived in the terms of some coherent ontological understanding, as well as existentially related to the patterns of our lived experience.

For Origen and Augustine on through its Thomistic culmination, the Catholic tradition has recognized this intrinsic and unavoidable relation between philosophical analysis and theological expression. Not only Catholic natural theology, but also the most intrinsically "religious" of its notions (for example that of the Eucharistic presence) has received in this tradition philosophical explication. The danger is that frequently this objectifying philosophical expression has overwhelmed and obscured both the eidetic, biblical meanings and the existential or personal "sense" of these symbols, as the Reformers rightly perceived. Nevertheless, Catholicism has been correct in insisting that Christian symbols must be able to be thought or conceived, for in order to assent to a symbol a man must be able to *conceive* it, and in order to conceive it he must understand it in relation to all else he knows and conceives in his experience. Consequently, any symbol must have an ontological as well as an eidetic and an existential meaning.

The ontology in terms of which we today understand our traditional symbols must, however, be a *modern* ontology. For we live and experience ourselves and our world in modern terms. If, therefore, Christian symbols can have meaning for us only as shapers of our experience of history and of ourselves, then by the same token we can think of them only in the same terms as we think of ourselves and our world, that is, in modern terms. We understand ourselves and our world in different terms than past ages did: experience and cognition, space and time, substance, contingency, relatedness, causality, temporality, and autonomy—each of these fundamental categories has for us an inescapably modern character. And any religious symbols inclusive of them that we can regard as true, as relevant to and ultimately formative of *our* world, must share the contours of this modern ontology that is ours. No theology based on an ontology from another age, expressive of a different experience of the world and thus of different ways of thinking of that world, can be alive in our existence or function in our fundamental thought. It is this valid point that lies back of the insistence of "liberal" Catholicism that Catholic doctrines must be freed from their traditional Thomistic basis and rethought in the terms of some modern philosophy.

It is not enough for theological reflection (as now I must confess I once thought)[6] to relate the eidetic meaning of the symbol to lived, existential experience in order for us to conceive it. For a theological symbol to become a doctrine for our reflection, it must be expressed in modern ontological and philosophical form. Thus, as I noted in the preceding chapter, the results of modern philosophical analysis, as well as those of modern scientific analysis, impinge on and in turn shape the meaning for us of the religious symbols in terms of which we organize, understand, and deal with our experience. Inevitably, therefore, those traditional theologies that explicitly and implicitly depend on ontologies, which, like the experience they reflect, stem from another age (in Protestant Lutheran or Calvinist orthodoxy, or in Catholic Thomism), are in that form irrelevant to us, and implicitly or explicitly each of their present-day creative representatives, in doing modern theology, transforms their fundamental symbolic statements into modern ontological terms.

This transformation is again "tricky" because it is creative, and so it too is a risk. The Christian symbol must rule the use we make of any modern ontology as a superior norm of expression, lest we proclaim a modern secular ontology as unequivocally Christian, and our gods be different than God. Thus no philosophical system per se, modern or Greek, can be adopted without transformation to fit the symbols of our tradition. There is, unfortunately, no available "method" to set secure rules for this use of metaphysics and ontology in theology. We can only try to do it, and hope for the best; that is, hope that our expression of Christian truth in modern and relevant ontological form is a faithful rendition of the Christian symbols, at least as faithful as that of the thirteenth century in Aristotelian form! Like every Christian, the theologian in his work can only pray for the help of the Spirit. But the issue must be joined. For as there is no *Christian* theology without Christian symbols drawn from the tradition, and no *relevant* or *healing* theology without the component of contemporary lived experience, so there can be no *conceptuality* or *thought* in the church without modern ontology.

# Chapter V

## *The Origins of Action in Theological Understanding*

THE PRECEDING CHAPTERS speak of methods in theology, and in that process emphasize the grave difficulties that our modern secular culture poses for us, almost as if that culture were too powerful and stable to be challenged, and surely too permanent to be ignored. Yet when we look up from our office desks and peer into the streets, another scene appears. There we see the culture itself in deep turmoil. Rumblings of fundamental change and even of revolution are heard on every horizon; all the certainties of the secular world around us (like those of Catholicism within)—our moral, political, social norms, and even our scientific consciousness—are radically questioned, and not only by other societies around the globe (and we are the "dinosaurs" of our era) but by large sections of our own culture, especially our youth. Historical change, not contradictions in our psyches, is our deepest current problem; and the unknown shape of the future of a culture in turmoil is our burning concern. For our culture as well as our church is immersed in transition, caught in a tide rip of historical change. A cry for help arises from the very culture whose seeming power and stability appeared about to snuff out the church and even Christianity itself.

Perhaps the deepest irony of our time is that precisely

when modernity had eradicated (or sought to eradicate) symbols of ultimacy, that is, religious symbols, it has found itself most desperately in need of them. For if we are driven to historical consciousness, to consciousness of the future, to acting politically, then we need symbols of ultimacy with which these intense reactions can be illumined, strengthened, tempered, and guided. We need credible grounds for repentance and hope, and guides for creative action. A rupture in history, then, is one origin of action for us. And historical action means politics. The current political theologies are right: to be human at all, and *a fortiori* to be a Christian, and most of all to be a theologian, requires that our existence and our theology be political. For politics is the handle with which most directly men seek to grasp and creatively to direct historical change. History becomes an overwhelming Fate for those who attempt neither to comprehend nor morally to guide it.

Thus a fourth level of meaning for theological symbols has appeared: the ethical and political meaning. I have distinguished an "eidetic" sense intrinsic to a symbol or cluster of symbols, their experiential or existential meaning or sense in terms of lived experience, and their ontological meaning as basic concepts systematically related to our other fundamental concepts. And now I seek to emphasize their ethical and political meaning. All four are essential for theological understanding.

Orthodox Catholic and Protestant theology has as a whole been content with only the biblical and/or the ontological meanings of our major traditional symbols, that is, with their objective and precise dogmatic and metaphysical character. Both have tended to leave out their experiential meanings and their political implications, and the resultant lack is widely apparent. However biblical or creedal her dogmatic language, any "apolitical" church speaking for an "apolitical" theology (and most conservative forms of Catholicism and Protestantism sought to be just this) contradicts the meanings of her own most fundamental symbols, and thus destroys the integrity of her own existence as a church. For an apolitical religion or church, in remaining aloof from cultural, social, and political issues, does not thereby safeguard its transcendence in relation to the world. On the contrary, it relinquishes precisely that transcendance. Unintentionally or intentionally, such a church becomes a prophet of Mammon and of Caesar, not of Jahweh and the Cross. A sacramental blessing of the troops and the bombers is, as it has been since the days when the god Marduk rode before the armies of Assyria, as much a *political* act as is marching in the streets in protest against the war. A church, so long as it exists at all, functions politically, negatively or positively; it can hardly avoid a political meaning to all its actions in its world, whether they are intentionally political or not. In the same way and for the same reason, our theological reflections cannot avoid the ethical and political meanings of any of our most fundamental theological symbols. Otherwise the inescapably political actions of the church will fail to be guided by its Christian symbols and find themselves inspired solely by the other lesser "gods" of property, personal well-being, and racial or national security. Modern eschatological theology, at least in Jürgen Moltmann and Johannes B. Metz, tends to be content with only the eidetic biblical or traditional meanings and the political meanings, and so in its own way tends to be inadequate. But at least, like the American social gospelers, so long unheard in Tübingen and Münster, Moltmann and Metz are right to challenge churchmen to political consciousness and action, and our theological understanding to emphasizing the political meanings of all we say in faith.

Theological symbols, however, cannot be given a political and ethical meaning *ab extra*. That must be intrinsic to their eidetic meaning if they are to function genuinely as origins of creative action. Otherwise—as has so often been the case in church history—Christian political judgments and acts stem from other interests and sources, and Christian theology functions only to bless and sanctify causes that it neither originates nor criticizes. In terms of our analysis: in what sense are the political, ethical, and social meanings of theological symbols intrinsic to them? Or, to turn the question around, how is it that theological convictions expressed in symbols are genuine origins of creative action?

Every mythical and religious vision implies action of some sort. For one of the main functions of the myths and the religious symbols that structure the life of a culture is to express a vision of authentic man and woman, and thereby to make legitimate, and obligatory, the fundamental roles that people adopt in the culture's life: king, warrior, priest, farmer, fisherman, husband, wife, father, mother, and child. But not all mythical symbols are ethical and political in quite the sense I have implied. Many —and ours have often done this and frequently continue so to do—serve merely to adapt the person to the overarching cultural system in which he or she lives. They neither ground nor inspire creative actions of a *new* sort leading to a new, less distorted cultural and historical world. Such action is that for which both our times and our Christian symbols call. It is part of my argument that, as Ernst Bloch has so eloquently documented, authentic religion, and especially biblical religion, has more than any other factor been an important origin of such creative moral and political action.

If we ask why biblical symbols, and expressed through them authentic Christian religion, have this intrinsic relation to creative ethical and political action, there are, of course, many answers. The obvious one is that in our tra-

132 Catholicism Confronts Modernity

dition God is known to be righteous and moral, and calls man in turn to be moral. But this answer begs the question again, for all religions call on men and women to be moral as the religion in question defines morality. So the question is left unanswered about why Christian morality takes *this* form and thus has an intrinsic relation to creative political action.

One could begin almost anywhere, for every important Christian symbol points to ethical and political meanings of this sort. But I prefer in this discussion to emphasize a general dialectical character of all Christian symbols, what we may call their teleological or *unstable* character, their dual emphases on what has been and is and yet also what *should* and *will* be in the future. They all begin in an affirmation of something presently real and valuable, but they do not stop there. They move on, transcend themselves, and so point beyond what is to a further completion. They are thus essentially dynamic, historical, teleological, eschatological, and everything said or talked about in Christian faith has this unstable, "moving-beyond-itself" character. The transcendent is not only the source and ground of the present, but is also transcendent as "out in front" of the present as its goal; God is Alpha *and* Omega.

The fundamental symbols concerning man have this character. Basic among them is the *imago dei*, the affirmation that man is created as real and of value. He exists, therefore, as a person, free, rational, and creative, and so of worth because he has been made in the image of God. But this is no empirical statement, based on a survey of any of us as we are. As St. Irenaeus, St. Augustine and Kierkegaard have argued, this is not simply a description of man as if he were a stable substance that *has* this character, as water *is* $H_2O$. The image of God is also a task, a call to be what we are and yet even more what we are not, or are not yet. Man's humanity is as much something yet to be realized as it is the fundamental or essential structure of his being. Thus we are led to other fundamental and balancing symbols about man: for example, that at present he is a sinner; he has distorted his nature; and so he is unworthy. For Christians, therefore, the human self is not a substance or essence; it is an existence; it becomes through decision; it must will itself to be itself. Its being, therefore, is a project into the future, a creative task, a dynamic movement made up of inward decision and commitment on the one hand and of outward behavior, action and relations to others on the other, a project stretching unstably over time from past through present into the future.

Finally, the symbol of man as a new creature, what Tillich called "the new being," completes this emphasis on movement forward by expressing the goal, the deep *possibility* inherent in the Christian view of man. Through the work of divine grace, man becomes or will become fully man. Free of his past bondage to self and its concerns, he thus realizes his created nature to its fullest possibility through existing and acting in the future in trust in God, in loving relations with his fellows, and in hope for that future. Faith, hope, and love define man by specifying his *possibility* for the future under grace, a possibility that can only be realized or incarnated in actions in his world directed at a better future. Christian symbolism calls man into the future and into action in the world if he would become himself at all. The reality of the human self is thus teleological in form, a historical series of deeply related events leading to a completion in concrete existence and action. The self is a story, a history with a goal; and decision, commitment, and action are essential parts of that story.

The same active movement into the future is even more true of Christian symbols expressive of the being and nature of God. God is in truth being, the source of our being, and thus in some sense unoriginate, permanent, and ever-lasting; the eternal ground of whatever is real, true, and of value. But Jahveh is also an "unstable" being if ever there was one. He has fundamental purposes for man and for history; he acts in new ways to achieve those purposes. "Faithful" to what he intends, yet in that faithfulness he tears down what has been and institutes new covenants and new relations with men. Continually he judges what is, and always he calls men to what is not yet. Above all, throughout the scripture he promises a fulfillment of man's life and of history itself that is not yet visible. There is no utterance of the divine Word in the Old Testament that does not call men to a *new* existence and does not thereby set off a dynamic train of historical events leading to a *new* goal. And there is no appearance of the divine Word in the New Testament that does not point men, and even God himself, forward to death, resurrection, and final completion.

In the light of this essentially *dynamic* character to the symbolic account of man and of God, how strange it is that most of the Christian tradition has insisted on speaking of both in stable rather than unstable, static rather than dynamic terms, of a changeless, immortal soul and a changeless, eternal God. And in the light of the fact that this dynamic teleology points to a transformation of natural, individual, and historical life, a transformation referring to the *future* of that natural and historical life, how strange it is that this teleology has been interpreted almost exclusively as referring to another existence and another realm distinguished from the material world and the temporal history that God creates and rules. No wonder our ethical and political speech have been filled at best with contradictions and confusions, and at worst with sanctifying applause for what is in the world and not what might be. Through the strange workings of divine providence, the dynamic and the natural-temporal emphases of the modernity we share have made us in the church able, almost for the first time, to see with clarity these aspects of our own biblical and traditional symbolism.

Our most fundamental symbols of God and man thus point beyond the realities they posit to a further future reality, to be made manifest through divine and human actions alike. Affirmation of the divine grounding in the present and gratitude for gifts in the past are balanced by divine judgment and calling; acceptance in grace is balanced by promise; and all alike indicate a final fulfillment. The divine and the human realities to which our symbols point, which they communicate, and so which they realize in experience, are presently real and of value; and yet they are unstable and dynamic to their core. To exist in *this* world formed by these symbols is to be affirmed, challenged, and called in one's being, and thus compelled to action and oriented to the future. It is to be made in one's existence at once unstable and creative; it is to be grounded, accepted, strengthened, and rendered confident in that instability.

This essential instability of Christian symbols pointing beyond themselves—both for God and man and so for their common meeting place, history—is expressed in perhaps the most fundamental symbol of Jesus' teaching, the Kingdom to come; and in turn it expresses the great truth in contemporary eschatological theology that centers itself around that symbol. Everything we speak of in Christian theology is dynamic and historical, oriented toward its completion in the future. Hence all—God, creation, man, revelation, Christ, and history—are to be understood in terms of their end, the goal toward which they all point. History, politics, and eschatology are thus uneasy but natural companions unified in this symbol of the Kingdom; and all relevant theology today must be constructed in their terms.[1]

If one adds to this essentially temporal, dialectical, dy-

namic, and unsettling character of all Christian symbols
the other trait of the crucial symbols of biblical religion,
namely their *moral* character, one can see how intrinsically authentic commitment and theological understanding alike lead to ethical and political action. This moral
tone to each Christian concept is variously expressed: in
the communal nature and responsibility of man if he is to
be at all; in his responsibility inwardly to his neighbor; in
the character of authentic humanity and so of authentic
community as characterized by justice and love because
*this* is the completion of man's natural and historical
being as God has created him and as God thus wills his
fulfillment. The movement of God through history, and
the consequent movement of man beyond himself and beyond what history and society presently are, both have as
their goal a *moral* completion: the Kingdom of God,
which is a Kingdom of justice and love.

Thus the dynamic being and the moral intentions of
God: what is ultimately real and sacred express the instability of Christian reality and its moral goal. One cannot
serenely enter that world without commitment, decision,
and action; and one cannot live long in that world, encompassing individual *and* community, selves *and* history,
without being political. And both Jahveh and his prophets
*were* political. For both sought to shape the historical
process in which human selves might become what they
are to be. The basic biblical dialectics of dynamic reality
and moral completion, of individual and community, of
personal selves and historical process, whose interrelations penetrate deeply into every biblical symbol, make
this a political religion. They also make it the only cluster
of symbols of ultimacy capable of understanding the mystery of our historical being as our age views that mystery.

It is interesting and ironic that one of the major
grounds for the rejection of Christian symbolism in eigh-

teenth-century France (in its Roman Catholic forms) and in nineteenth-century Germany (in its Lutheran forms) was its sterile and conservative, if not demonic, political influence. If, asked the French philosophes and the German Young Hegelians alike, these Christian symbols bless every present form of corrupt power, if what is presently real in social life is thus identified with the divine ideal and so made sacred, how can man be ethical and creative? How can the real be transformed, which is the goal of creative moral action and politics, if what is now and what ought to be are united in a God who ordained both? This critique was sounded successively by Francis Bacon, Diderot, Condorcet, Voltaire, Feuerbach and Marx, and subsequently by a host of their liberal and Marxist followers, the greatest of whom in our day have been John Dewey and Ernst Bloch. That this critique was justified is a sad commentary not only on the sins of the church against her own message but also on her radical misunderstanding of the form and meaning of that message.

But the irony has deepened in our own day. For with the exception of what we will subsequently call the "renegade" Marxists, the two traditions that these eighteenth- and nineteenth-century critics of Christianity fathered—the empirical, naturalistic tradition and the Marxist tradition—have in our day themselves ended up in the same dilemma, namely, the identification of the real and the ideal, only now on a secular, empirical basis in the West, and on an established socialist basis in most of the Communist countries. We shall confine our discussion, although relevant to both the liberal West and the Marxist Russian sphere, to the former.

The essence of the empirical tradition, begun in the Enlightenment and becoming more radical ever since, has been that, first, all relevant and valid thinking must eschew symbols of ultimacy, religious symbols, and even transcendent moral norms, and accommodate itself to

what is immediately and empirically given, to a study and
an understanding of what can be observed in the present
and tested in the immediate future; secondly, that the
achievement of such empirical truth and its use in action
involves the manipulation of the object of inquiring
thought in line with the immediate goals and purposes of
the inquirer. Empirical study and purposive manipulation
are the twin canons of present knowing and doing, and
their consequence has been a culture dominated by scientific techniques of knowing and technical modes of action
and control. The irony is that, like the theological tradition they overthrew, they too in the end have stifled creative ethical and political action in history. The reason is
that they also overlook the dialectic expressed in the biblical symbols. The final irony is that in this argument for
the continuing relevance of Christian symbolism, I am
indebted to three "renegade" Marxists, Ernst Bloch, Herbert Marcuse, and Jürgen Habermas—"renegade" because
they all see the application of this critique, not only to the
liberal, empirical West, but also to established Communism
in its Russian form.

To define the truth as the accommodation of thought to
what is immediately or empirically real, to what is ob-
servable and present at hand, is, argued Bloch, to miss the
main purpose of creative thinking. That purpose, and so
the real criterion for creative thinking, is to change what
is into what is not yet, to transform reality into what it
might and should be.[2] Thus the most significant human
thinking has represented what are precisely *not* "the
facts," but what is not yet, the ideal that is not yet actual
but might be. Without this transcendent dimension, our
thinking is confined to the parameters of present history
and can never break out of them. In the social sciences,
for example, in order for that inquiry to be "empirical"
and nothing else, the present system alone is investigated,
its role and structures studied and outlined, its modes of

adaptation and of value consequently implicity accepted. If, however, thought remains thus "empirical," no possible challenge to the sacrality of the present is possible. The structures of process and of change away from the present are in principle not understood; and the rational norms of what should be if history is to fulfill itself are a priori excluded from attention and analysis.[3] Empiricism is therefore itself an ideology, sanctifying the present because it is unable—and perhaps ultimately unwilling[4]—to rise beyond the present to be critical of it and constructive in relation to it. The "instability," the thrust forward, generated by the divine judgment on what is, the divine calling to transform what is, and the divine goal in a more perfect Kingdom of love and justice, is lacking here. The "new" in history is thus foreclosed as nonadaptive, therefore irrational and immoral, and creative political action dies in the mazes and harmonies of a sacred system.

Correspondingly, as Marcuse has argued,[5] to define valid knowing exclusively as manipulation of its object is to divest the objects of knowledge of every *intrinsic* reality and worth for themselves. Since objects *are* for us only insofar as we experience and then know them, objects that are known only through manipulation *are* for us only as functions of our manipulating analysis. Their reality for our thought is their behavior in response to our manipulation; for all we can know of them is so discovered and so defined. Thus man known in this way becomes an object divested of any intrinsic worth, and therefore so conceived as to be a *fit* object of our manipulative purposes. Understood merely as an objective mechanism, man can appropriately be controlled and refashioned, as is nature in traditional technology, according to the will of the technologist, and ultimately, therefore, according to the will of the latter's political bosses. Such a total view of man, endemic to the empirical social sciences, leads not only to the acceptance of the present social system, but even fosters the worst elements of that system. For it understands the object of rational thought: man, as merely an objective element or particle in a wider natural and social system; and it understands the purpose of that thought to be to adapt man more harmoniously to the requirements of that social order in which he is understood, and therefore to the requirements of those who rule and profit from that order.

There is so much truth in this critique it is painful. And it helps explain why many of the liberal elements in our culture—originally committed to creative political action and dynamic change—could have, through their roles as scientific students of society, become conservative in their attitudes and above all in their effects; they became an instrument and justification of the total system of our social life, and therefore sterile and in some cases demonic, as was the church, in political life. As the church, through its sacred dogmas and holy charismas, was once all too often the agent of spiritual sanctification of the dubious social order of *its* day in the name of the divine transcendence, so ironically can contemporary social science, precisely through the "secular" and so the empirical and manipulative character of its understanding of truth, perform the same ambiguous role.

What is lacking is precisely the dialectic I outlined earlier. On the one hand there is needed the affirmation of the reality and value of being, nature, and man, in themselves as natural forms of being and as persons. Such an affirmation of the inherent *integrity* and *value* of nature and of persons underscores the ultimate impossibility and inappropriateness of their manipulation by an observer. Knowledge of their deepest reality and their inherent worth arises, as Tillich said, not through technique but only through participation, union, empathy, and ultimately through love. On the other hand, what is needed is also the understanding of man and of society, not only in present, empirical terms (what they appear now in history to be) but also in terms of what they *might* be, of the goal toward which their being and activity are directed, the ideal which is the *telos* of their reality and so an aspect of its essential nature. Again this presupposes a different mode of understanding than the merely empirical, a mode qualified again by participation and union but also structured by symbols of ultimacy that refer to the possibilities of the future, an *eschatological* understanding based on the promise latent in what now is. In our secular and religious life we need a wider view of the powers of human knowing than an empirical culture provides. And we need symbols of ultimacy expressive both of the deeper substantial reality of what is and of the ontological significance of possibility, of the not yet, of what is still to be.

Above all, such an empirical mode of analysis and understanding, confined to observations and manipulations, has no way at all to deal with the horizon of ultimacy in which man lives. It can, therefore, find no powers greater than those of pragmatic reason and purposive manipulation as the principles of meaning and control in history, and therefore no ground except man's practical wisdom and moral good sense on which to base its hope for future. But such ultimate confidence in man as knower and manipulator, as scientist and technologist, immerses the modern consciousness in an implacable and ruthless fate of its own creation—the given social system, an accelerating technology, a political history not amenable to easy pragmatic manipulation—either from the laboratory or from Washington. And thus in confining man to his own perceptual present, it imprisons him within an historical moment that he has not created and so in a historical process that he cannot finally control, a process that consequently he can only fear.

This discussion represents by no means a claim that

biblical symbols alone are the origins of creative political
action; nor does this argument for their usefulness in relation to the problems of historical life represent a conclu-
sive proof of their validity. But it may help us to see the
vast relevance of these symbols to politics and the deeper
issues of history. At any rate, it is clear that creative ethical and political action needs more than empirical knowledge and technical know-how. Also, dialectical symbols
are needed, expressive of the reality and value of nature,
man, and history, and also of the transcendent source and
ground of history's motion, and of the open possibilities
that the future offers. Creation, judgment, and the promise of redemption are not symbols referring to another
realm far beyond the natural, historical, social, and personal world of our present experience. Rather, they provide the most meaningful and valid structuring of our
present natural, historical, and personal existence, and
thus the most stable ground for hope in their fulfillment.

Futurist theology, the political theology of eschatology
dominant in contemporary Protestantism and Catholicism
alike, arose because of these two criticisms: first of the
sterility of traditional theology with its omnipotent God
sanctifying the present, and then the critique of liberal
empiricism as also sanctifying the present. As Ernst Bloch
taught these "new" theologians, the future can be opened
for new possibility—and without *that* how can there be
creative politics?—only if God is not the omnipotent ruler
of the present, and if the "not yet," the "possible" in the
future, is recognized as the center of inspiration, the sacred object of thought, action, and hope. Thus God was
moved out of the present into the future, and the radical
politics of change made union with biblical eschatology.
The new is possible for our weary and tortured world
because, says this theology, God is the God of the future,
appearing out of future possibilities to negate and then to

master a decaying and unjust present with his totally new creation fulfilling his ancient promise. Much of current Christian political activity, Protestant and Catholic alike, finds the religious and theological origins of its action in this eschatological vision.

I have indicated already my agreement in large part with a good deal of this potent form of present theology: the necessity of political meaning and action if biblical and Christian symbols are to be authentically understood and embodied; the forward, eschatological tension of all biblical symbols; and finally the legitimate critique of both traditional theology and liberal empiricism for their implicit, and all too effective, conservative bias. I believe, however, that an exclusively eschatological theology—one in which all crucial symbols are interpreted solely in eschatological terms—is self-defeating and self-contradictory; and that it has difficulty, despite its power, in providing on its own a symbolic horizon suitable for creative political action in the present. I shall briefly indicate here three of the reasons why I think it truer to the meaning of the biblical symbols, the internal coherence of theology, and the needs of politics to balance the God of the future, eschatology, with the activity of God in the historical present, with the symbol of providence.

An exclusively eschatological theology, in which God's being and activity are solely future and not present, leaves our present, and so the social world in which we exist and our inward experience of that world, barren of divine activity, and therefore empty of all experience of the divine dimension within which we exist. In such a world, barren of God's presence, all social movement from latency and potentiality in the present into actuality in the future, that is, all *political* activity, is ipso facto severed from relationship to God's activity. For political activity works precisely with the latencies of the present, grasping them in understanding and then in action (praxis) in order to bring forth from them what is creatively possible. If God works *solely* from the future, he cannot be the ground of and related to our political work, which depends on these pregnancies of the present. Our political action has, therefore, a purely "secular" and in no way a divine ground, and a political *theology* has no real referent or meaning.

Politics is the art of grasping and utilizing the possible latent within the present. It is creative only if it directs and uses forces presently at work in social actuality. Any political action, whether conservatively preserving or radically changing the old, will be infinitely frustrated and destructive if there are no such "latencies" for it to grasp and use. If the old is in fact dead, to seek to preserve it is hopeless and infinitely destructive; if the new is not in fact at all possible, action to bring it into actuality is either totally abortive or itself again infinitely destructive. Creative politics depends on comprehending and using what is latently but *really* there. As Bloch says, tendencies latent in the present, with which the present is pregnant, provide on the historical level essential conditions for any genuine possibilities of the future. The total ground of political action, as of movements into a creative future, is thus constituted not only by "future possibility" but also by historical destiny, that which the present has inherited from the past and which it will shape into a new future. Political action, which seeks to direct this pregnancy of history's present, is thus always essentially related to what has been and to what is presently actual. This is true even of revolutionary politics, which builds negatively on the contradictions and tensions of the present, and positively on the new possibilities latent within that disturbed present. Marx understood this very well, and balanced the not-yet of possibility with the inevitable working within past and present of the material dialectic out of whose slowly developing processes the utopian possibilities would eventually arise. Thus no creative political action can totally repudiate the structures and latencies of the present, and base its confidence entirely on what is utterly new, on what is solely transcendent to the present in the future. If, then, social and historical changes, however radical, are built on what is *there*, and if creative political action is based on latencies in the present, any political theology must in turn ground its activity and its relevance on the work of God in past and present, not only on his work "from the future." Otherwise the *political* judgments of an eschatological theology (based on a consciousness of the needs and possibilities of what is in the present) will be divorced from its theological affirmations (based on what God has promised or will do in the future), and the theology, as political theology, will be incoherent. Eschatology must fulfill, not negate, God's providence, if it is to have implications for present action, that is, political relevance.

If the present is devoid of God's activity, except as promise, then a political theology can have as little theological *meaning* as it has political relevance. If our present world is in fact devoid of the divine presence and work, then inescapably our present experience is barren of any experience, negative or positive, of the divine. In such a situation there can be no "sense," no experiential meaning, to any theological concepts or symbols at all. For theological symbols have meaning (have "sense") to us only if they thematize aspects of our ordinary and present experience; and they have "use" only if they shape the structure of the present world in which we have our being and in which we must act. In a totally secular present horizon, experience becomes devoid of any facet of ultimacy or sacrality; past, present, and future are thus equally barren of transcendence and deity; and there is no way from an utterly secular present to *mean* a "religious" future. The meaning for us now of eschatological symbols about the future thus presupposes at the minimum a prethematized but real "sense" to these symbols in God's action in deep but real *present* experience of ultimacy, a "preontological ontology," an awareness of the sacred as grounding and yet in contradiction to our present. But such a divine presence in the present, grounding the possibilities of our meaningful work toward God's future, is precisely God's hidden but real activity in the present, which has been "named" by the symbol of providence. An eschatological language, as well as an eschatological politics, presupposes the present work of God, our experience of that work, and our response to it.

Political action—even political action by idealists—is always partial and ambiguous, a part of the history of sin as well as of the history of grace. To believe that this ambiguity is true of our opponents and not of ourselves, that with *our* radical political action a wholly new era of virtue and love will be ushered in, is to be in danger of fanaticism, intolerance, and in the end cruelty to all who do not share our vision. Pardoxically, any such close identification of *our* action with the ultimate possibilities of God's future will in fact only extend into that future the history of sin arising out of past and present; and so it will succeed only in delaying that future as each preceding generation has done. Human action is relative and partial, and the more it claims God's ultimacy for itself, the further from the divine goal it moves. Eschatology as a category, however, inescapably implies such ultimacy. An eschatological symbol by its very nature points to God's "final" act, the ultimate manifestation of God's being and his purposes, not their hidden, proximate, preliminary manifestations. When God's "eschatological action" is referred to, therefore, a new era utterly different from the old is immediately and inescapably implied. Now to believe that such an era is to dawn as the future moves into our present may conceivably be argued to be sound biblical theology; but to associate, or worse to identify, that ultimate movement of God's future too directly with our own political action in meeting that future, is fatal politically, morally, and religiously. It is to confound the ambiguity of our political actions in the moving present with the ultimacy and clarity of God's eschatological deed from the future; and that is precisely the ground and meaning of fanaticism. Far from appearing in history as the pure instruments of God's final redemptive action, our ambiguous but important political actions will be met *also* by God's judgment; and the more so when we feel that they represent his will unequivocally and finally. It is the hidden, secret, limited (self-limited, to be sure), "providential" activity of God in continuing history, an activity that preserves, judges, and uses the waywardness of human freedom to create the ambiguity of the past and the present, to which our present political activity most directly relates; not God's final, unambiguous, and culminating activity associated with eschatology. Certainly, that hidden activity, which traditionally has been called providence, has God's ultimate purposes at *its* goal; thus in turn providence must be understood and defined eschatologically. However, the divine activity that our political actions supplement and in part help to effect, cannot for us be the *ultimate*, eschatological activity of God, manifesting at last his final purpose, lest we become more demonic than we are. Rather, what our political actions supplement is God's hidden providence working in the world, which grounds all our actions, but which also combines with his judgment as much as with our virtue to bring about creative change.

As I have noted throughout this volume, change is basic to the reality of history and of social existence. Hence creative action in history, political action, takes place in relation to change, resisting some forms of change and encouraging others. To understand change *solely* eschatologically—as the instrument of God's ultimate act from the future—is to misunderstand historical process and to distort political action in relation to that process. The reason historical reality is *process* is that every present is pregnant with change, and thus with new possibilities for the future. Change therefore implies a dynamic relation of possibility to present actuality; in turn, to act politically is to grasp and direct that dynamic relation between present actuality and future possibility. The *immediate* locus of meaning in historical change, and in politics, is found, therefore, in the interrelation between present actuality and future possibility, and in the development of that latency into the realization of new possibility—not solely in the reverse relation of the future and its ultimate possibility to the present, even though in that ultimate future the end of the process is seen. Both process and goal are important in understanding and coping with historical change. Consequently, both providence and eschatology express symbolically the relation of God's activity to our history and our activity in that history. If we are to have confidence amid radical change—a very difficult but necessary achievement for creative politics—it is not only because we know the ultimate future of God, but also because we know that in the confusion and ambiguity of the present, there is a latency pregnant with creative possibilities, a divine providential power at work in time and change. It is this present but hidden activity to which our politics is related, though it is to God's final self-manifestation and goal that our actions are finally directed. Again, eschatological politics requires as its own ground a politics based on God's providential work in the past and present.

For all these reasons it seems to me that the origin of Christian action lies in a dialectical interrelation of symbols rather than in one eschatological cluster: an unstable dialectic between God's present and his future work, between the creative, affirming, judging, and calling work of God in the historical present—his providential work—and the promise of his completion in the goal of history and of life—his eschatological fulfillment.

This work of providence in public or social history, so crucial to political and personal action, is "hidden." Neither the reality nor the direction of the divine activity in our institutional life is easily or clearly visible, especially in Washington! Thus, when we seek to describe what we are calling the public work of providence, it is not easy to say how it is to be located in our social experience. To answer, then, the questions: "Where and how is God at work in the world?" and "How do we find out where and how God is at work?," we must turn to other aspects of our experienced relation to God, to other symbols. For providence in historical public life is *hidden*, in both the divine self-limitation that allows us freedom and in the waywardness of our political actions that combine with his providence. However, if my analysis is right, and if political action is related to the "public" work of providence, the answer to the question "Where is God at work in our world" is crucial as the primary theological ground for both our political norms and our political action. If no such divine ground is there in the present, our actions, based as they are on present forces and possibilities, will be determined only by "secular" norms and possibilities. Thus despite the hidden character of God's present activity, the definition of the *character* of providence, the kind of work God does and is doing in our world, is essential for a Christian politics, in both secular and ecclesiastical affairs. To discover what it is that God is doing in his church, to *understand* what the relation is between changing ecclesiastical forms and the divine presence and purposes, is to be able to act effectively in ecclesiastical issues. Correspondingly, to discover what God is doing in his world, to understand the relation of changing institutional and social forms to the divine presence and purposes in history, is to have praxis and so to be able to act effectively, and in a Christian manner, in politics.

Certainly one of the major sources for such a definition, or criterion, of the work of providence lies in eschatology; for eschatological symbols express the content of the divine promises concerning God's ultimate goal, summed up in the symbol of the Kingdom of God. However, since we cannot yet experience that ultimate future, the content of the divine promises, and any present knowledge of God's ultimate goal we may now have, is in turn itself largely determined by what we know of God in past events and in our present experiences of the meaning of those past events. The divine Word to which scripture bears witness —as it appears in the entire covenant with Israel, and as it reaches its culmination in the event of Jesus Christ—to my mind unquestionably provides the most fundamental basis for our knowledge of God's ultimate eschatological purposes and our criterion for discerning his providential work in the world. A thorough discussion of our theme, therefore, would begin *there*: in the divine promises from the beginning, the covenant and its meaning, the prophetic witness, the words, acts and resurrection of Jesus as witnessed to by the early community, and in the "promise" both articulated and implied in this entire tradition. However, in this brief and extremely incomplete discussion of eschatology and its relation to providence and ethics, I would like to keep as close touch with certain elements of the Catholic ethical tradition as I can, and thus to relate our knowledge of God's eschatological promises to our experiences in the present of *nature* and *grace*. These two are, to be sure, also ultimately to be interpreted and defined in the light of the Word; but here they will be considered as aspects of present experience that manifest to us now the character of the divine activity and purpose in that social world around us.

Thus in seeking to understand what God is "about" in

our world, we shall look at two aspects of present Christian experience: first of all, our personal experience of judgment, acceptance, and redeeming *grace* derived from our relation as individual human beings to the event of Jesus Christ, his words, actions, and total meaning communicated to us through the Word and the Spirit present in the community; second, our personal experience of the work of the divine in our ordinary, natural life as human beings in the world. There is an interrelation, a deep correlation, between the work of God in creating and sustaining our personal being and our natural life—a work we experience moment by moment in our ordinary, daily experience; the revelation of God's redeeming grace in Christ, through the Word and the Christian community; and the ultimate goal of God's creative and redemptive work in history in the eschatological future. This correlation expresses the consistency, faithfulness, and unity of God's being, activity, and intentions; it represents the fact that in turn both nature and grace, that is, every aspect of our human being and every dimension and stage in history—beginning, middle, and end—are equally grounded in God's being and work. And finally, it makes possible the understanding of his hidden providential work in public history in terms of these other "places" where he has manifested himself.

This correlation of creation, providence, revelation, redemption, and eschatology is the deepest *theological* reason that the traditional distinction between nature and supernature has to be reformulated *teleologically*. In creating and sustaining nature, God expressed the *same* purposes and goals as in his redemptive work of grace through Christ. Grace restores and perfects nature; it does not create something or some level of life transcendent to it. But "nature" and the redeeming grace that restores it are in turn to be understood providentially and eschatologically, that is, as a human nature and a human world

being led by God's providence to an eschatological fulfillment in this world as well as the next. The tradition of
natural law through which Catholic ethics have understood man and society, and so on which most Catholic
personal and political ethics have been based, has proved
useful in mediating God's ultimate will to common present social and personal experience. However, it understood that ultimate will in static terms, associating God's
law for the world first with the natural and social orders
perfectly embodied at the original creation (absolute natural law), and secondly with the orders relatively embodied in the world's traditional (or thought to be traditional) social and institutional forms (relative natural
law). My suggestion, in the light of these thoughts, is that
this tradition of natural law should be interpreted, not in
terms of either the original creation or of present social
experience, but rather reinterpreted teleologically and
eschatologically. Thus the "natural law" expressive of
God's will for man and history expresses a human being
and a human world directed toward their own natural
fulfillment in the Kingdom and in God. "Supernature" in
this view is not a second level higher than that of natural
life; the supernatural is here the ground of the *natural*,
the principle of its historical development and realization,
and the goal of its destiny. In turn, absolute natural law
points to the eschatological end of the process, not to its
origin, as eschatology points to the fulfillment of what is
natural and historical, not to its transcendence. Such a
providential and eschatological—a *teleological*—interpretation of natural law might give dynamic and radical,
rather than static and conservative, character to Catholic
ethics. What now is does not form the ultimate norm for
"nature"; rather, what now is is to be judged and transformed by God's ultimate goal. And this present activity
of judgment and transformation constitutes the character
and intention of God's present providential work in what

is. Such an interpretation of nature and natural law can, along with the divine activity of redemption, relate creation to eschatology as *stages* in or aspects of God's continuing historical activity instead of separating them into two different levels of present existence. Human nature, to be fully human, has the eschatological goal of God's Kingdom; human society, to be fully human, must fulfill the eschatological goal of the Kingdom of justice and love. Here supernature defines nature's possibilities; and thus a commitment to God sends a man or woman into the world in creative politics instead of translating them to another sphere.

In conclusion let us look briefly into these aspects of God's work: in our ordinary experience of our own being, in redemption through Christ, and in the eschatological promises, to see how we might define that most hidden of the modes of the divine activity (and yet most crucial for politics)—God's providential work in the social world around us and the criteria for our political action there. For in each of these areas there are clues, consistently similar in each area, to the divine activity amid our social history.

We experience the divine ground of our life in the wonder of our contingent being and in the security, vitality, and effectiveness of the life we owe to him. In our experience of grace through Christ this "natural" blessing of life is continued and exceeded in the eschatological promise of eternal life. Thus first of all we know that God works in the world to bring life, at every stage and level of its manifestation and promise; God is the Alpha and the Omega of life in all its creative form. And so wherever natural and social forces in community tend to increase the security of life for all, in them we know the hidden work of God as creative providence is at work. And in turn we know that we are called to act politically to eradicate whatever makes others insecure or in want, or threatens their life. Basic material justice as a political norm has its ultimate roots in the value of our human being and our life; it has its Christian norms in the activity of God to create and increase life. Thus it results politically in the requirement that this being and life, grounded in God and intended in its completion by him, be shared by all whom God has created. For such sharing is one facet of the divine goal.

We experience the divine in secular existence as the ground of the *meaning* of our life, the worth of what we do in community and with others, the eros, and the possibility of participating in common enterprises of value. And in the grace communicated to us through Christ we know this as the gracious gift of acceptance, reconciliation, and *koinonia*. Therefore, we know through our experience of nature and grace that God's providence works in the world to bring meaning, and participation in community. Whenever social structures are discovered that impede the meaning of life for men and women, or for some of them, and that hinder their participation in the values of their community, then these structures are opposed to God's work. And whenever social structures are devised that give place and participation, meaning and identity, to people in their common life, there the work of God is evident. Providence is the work of God that provides new forms and new possibilities of order and participation for the changing social life of men.

Finally, we experience the divine ground of our life through the exercise and reality of our autonomy and freedom, and the moral responsibility and personal inwardness that this exercise entails. This realization of our autonomy is superlatively experienced in redeeming grace through Christ, in the gifts of identity, commitment, and love that are the fruits of grace. Thus where communities grow with real individuals, with a measure of autonomy and freedom, with mutual respect and love, there the work of providence in history is discernible, a work in the world that is parallel to the work of creation and redemption experienced by us. And correspondingly, we are called politically to help fashion such communities. In sum, we can discern the work of providence in social history in the creation of social structures conducive of security, meaningful participation, community and freedom, because on the level of our ordinary life this is where we experience God, and in his redeeming grace this is what through Christ he seeks to realize for us. And through these criteria we can discern our political tasks in refashioning actuality toward this possibility defined by God's eschatological goal.

History is ambiguous, and we are wayward; our minds are unclear and our wills curve inwardly. But within our present there is a divine dimension at work creating, judging, and calling us toward the future. This hidden but essential reality is only dimly seen in personal experience, but it is more directly named in grace. And thus the character of its calling and the shape of its goals can be known to us. God is life and being, order and love, reconciliation and community. These he gives to us as the essential structures of our personal being, structures that are redeemed and perfected in grace. In the same way He calls us and the history we live in to creatively participate in his "public" work of sustaining and enriching life, molding higher forms of participation, and achieving deeper communities of freedom and love. The work of providence is defined eschatologically by the Kingdom; but the fulfillment of eschatology is achieved by our active, ethical, and political union in social action with the present, hidden activity of providence in the world. It is out of this unstable dialectic, and the symbols expressive of it, that the origins of our actions are located.

# Chapter VI

# *The Grammar of Assent*

IN THE PRECEEDING chapters I have tried to point to a fundamental dialectic involved in Christian theological understanding: myth and symbol with science and philosophy; traditional symbols and present experience; present reality and future possibilities for action. Now we come to the fourth dialectical theme: that of objectivity and rational argument in theology on the one hand, and of existential involvement and participation on the other. The general subject to which this dialectical applies is the issue of truth: how is the truth in theological understanding known to be true? What is the grammar of assent to its truth? What are its criteria?

Two poles have appeared and reappeared in this interminable discussion in Christian history. First, there are those who have emphasized the rational and objective side, and have pleaded for philosophical argument and understanding, for empirical, phenomenological, or logical argument, and even for "proof" in theology, and regarded the other side as hopelessly irrational, mystical, or fideist, private, and esoteric—as little better than sophisticated snake-handlers. Their reasons have been multiple; through rational argument alone do we *know* we deal in Christian faith with "reality"; with rational argument alone

are we in the present free as rational beings from the crush-
ing and often anachronistic authority of an uncritical
tradition (ecclesiastical or biblical)—two points deeply
felt by many contemporary Catholics. For them St. Voltaire and the Holy Spirit are almost one and the same.

The others have emphasized the need for personal experience, involvement, conviction, and decision: a fundamental *metanoia* or transformation in one's existence and
in one's religious existence, i.e., a change of self at the
deepest level, if Christian truth about God is to be known
and understood. For how can we speak intelligibly and
validly about God who is *Lord*, who searches the heart,
judges, and redeems, unless *we* inwardly recognize him as
Lord, repent, and have trust in him? Thus in the name of
the *Christian* character of Christian truth, they have emphasized revelation and faith, a prior inward acceptance
of the presence and authority of God, if the truth that
comes from God alone is to be known and understood. To
them their opponents in this matter are dry, intellectual
philosophers who have strayed from the academic reser-
vation, judging and editing a truth with their minds while
in fact that truth should judge and transform them: thus
they are desecrating matters of the sacred. For them St.
Voltaire and the Holy Spirit are polar opposites with no
possible mediation between them.

As is evident, I will argue that both are right and that
at every stage of theological understanding and the assent
to which it leads, rational understanding and participation, personal involvement, and faith radically interpenetrate each other so that neither side can develop without
the other. Only from their convergence does theological
understanding and its assent appear.

Christian commitment and reflection, first of all, have
always regarded their object as *the* truth, and so as the
truth, at least potentially, for all men: about man's exis-

tence, his world and God, and about past, present, and future. The biblical sources of this claim regarding truth, and the historical expressions of it, are too well known to belabor. It is, however, well to ponder its implications, for they point us powerfully toward the rational and objective pole of our subject. For truth, however we seek to understand it, is universal; it is of universal applicability and relevance in its domain, and in *intention* it commands or seeks to elicit universal assent. If it concerns man as man, and certainly if it concerns the God of all things, it applies to all men, under all conditions, and thus to the total range of human experience. Nothing in heaven and earth is or can be irrelevant to it, and, potentially, all that is experienced and known must be coherent with whatever in Christian affirmation claims to be the truth.

The difficulty here for the fideist's view of theology arises in the tension between the particularity of *his* truth and the universality of truth. If Christian truth is confined to special, involved religious experiences enjoyed by only one particular community of people, and if theology refuses coherently to relate its "truth" known in faith to other truths known outside that special experience and particular community, then Christian truth, which claims to be universal in character, is utterly divorced from all else that we regard as true, and from our usual means of arriving at the truth. For all of us, even the fideist, assume in most of our life that facts, evidence, and rational interpretation are relevant ways of arriving at the truth. Whatever our theological position, we conduct ourselves, or try to, as *rational* beings when we search for the truth; we assume a correlation between evidence, reason or argument, coherence, and the truth we seek. Thus it is difficult, not to say contradictory, for us to claim at one moment that Christianity is the truth of all truths, and yet is totally unrelated to our ordinary ways of arriving at the truth, to our serious reflections in common sense, in the sciences and in philosophy.

I have defined theological understanding as a delineation or thematization of general human existence by means of or through Christian symbols, an understanding of man's being in the world in *these* "Christian" terms—or as David Tracy puts it, an understanding of human existence in the light of the Christian fact. Clearly the intention of such reflection is to state a universally relevant truth, to provide an interpretation meaningful and valid for all human existence, to all men and women everywhere. Theology is not merely the understanding of the religious existence of the Christian community, as if its symbols clarified only the religious or Christian problems and questions peculiar to that historical group. Christian proclamation and its theological understanding in principle provide an interpretation of universal existence, of the problems, crises, and questions of all men and women everywhere, and an understanding, potentially if not in fact, of the joys, values, and hopes of *all* people.

If this is true about theology (and it is), two implications follow. First, theological understanding must be related to all sorts of facts and experiences, at least in principle. If it interprets *all* experience, not just special experiences, it must be coherently related to what we regard as *true* about all facets of experience, that is, to the sciences and other rational disciplines. But that coherent relation to truth otherwise known—to philosophy, science, and common sense—inevitably involves reason, a rational account of our religious symbols and their relations to other systems of symbols. Needless to say, this necessitates phenomenological analysis, analysis of language, epistemology, and ontology—the whole range of philosophical inquiry.

Second, theological understanding must be in principle

intelligible and meaningful to any person who is willing to ponder the evidence—and the evidence to which appeal is made must be available to him. Otherwise, theology is not (as every missionary claims it to be) an interpretation of *his* experience as well as of ours. Thus it must be stated so as to encompass and interpret what he finds in *his* world. For this reason I have argued for the necessity of an appeal to common, ordinary, general experience as men and women in our time have possessed that experience. Such ordinary daily experience could be called "natural" as opposed to "supernatural" experience. Thus because (as in the Catholic tradition) it is *reason*, i.e., some mode of philosophical analysis, that explores natural experience, there must be an intrinsic relation of theological understanding to philosophy. If our religious symbols interpret and thematize natural and not supernatural experience, theology, as understanding of natural experience through *Christian* symbols, must be in direct correlation with philosophical reason as the means by which natural experience is analyzed. If this is so, and if philosophical and theological understanding in this way radically interpenetrate each other, then the canons of theological inquiry and the criteria of its validity must include the canons of philosophy itself. As one mode of human cognition—and that it must be if we are to *know* by its means—theology is bound by the criteria of rational inquiry appropriate to issues of general or universal truth, namely, adequacy to and applicability in the entire range of human experience, and the systematic coherence of its most fundamental concepts.

Finally, the intrinsic role of rational argument and explication in theology can be seen when we explore the meaning of assent, at least as assent is interpreted in contemporary theology. If religious assent is real, it must spring from the personal decision and conviction of each person. Otherwise it is not assent but submission, not personally knowing or inwardly believing but parrotting or mechanically repeating. We cannot say: "I have no idea myself what it means or whether it be true, but I accept it because the church (or the Bible, or the preacher) states it to be true." Our modern understanding of intellectual autonomy and integrity forces us all to assert as true only what to us—to our minds, our understanding of existence, and our interpretation of our experience—is meaningful and true. This radical requirement that all true assent be autonomous, that is, on the basis of our experience, insight, reflective judgments, and self-awareness through *our own* rational powers, has been most powerfully expressed in our time by Bernard Lonergan. Therefore, whatever is to be declared as true by Christians must be to them coherent, intelligible, and valid. It must be in accord with whatever else they hold to be true, and coherent with the evidence and right reason as they understand them.

The rational, objective pole of theological understanding thus has a multiple base: in the claim of Christianity to state and express a *universal* truth, in the task of theology to interpret the entire range of ordinary or *"natural"* human experience, and finally in the meaning of assent as *personal conviction* of the truth of whatever is affirmed.

One immediate implication of this characteristic of theological understanding is that the old distinction between confessional or dogmatic theology and apologetical theology dissolves. If to be Christian and to be affirmed at all theology must be seen as *true*, and as related coherently to all else that is held to be true, then the effort to relate theological symbols to the common ground of all human experience is *essential* to theology, and not merely a requirement of its proclamation to unbelievers. In order for dogmatic theology to become theological *understanding*, it must agree with the secular understanding in our own minds, and find common ground in the world of secular truths in which we all now live: it must be "apologetic" in character. Also dissolved is any stark distinction between philosophy and theology, as if the first dealt rationally with general human experience and the second, on quite other grounds unrelated to common experience or arguments about experience, with dogma. There may be good "political" reasons, in the mysteries of ecclesiology and academia, for this radical separation of philosophy from theology; but there are no longer any reasons in principle, or in the character of the present understanding of theology, for this sharp separation.

Rational argument on the basis of some common ground is, moreover, essential to every phase of theological work, and to each step or stage of theological assent. In the hermeneutical phase of theological understanding —when the meaning of the fundamental symbols of the tradition is uncovered, delineated, and interpreted—there must be objective historical and hermeneutical arguments based on the texts of scripture and tradition, and on a defensible method of interpreting these texts. No one can simply claim here that because they are "in the Spirit," or because he is bishop, or because the Curia (or Denzinger) insist on this interpretation, that *this* is the meaning, say, of *creatio ex nihilo*, original sin, the deity of Christ, or the eschatological promises. He must show this in accordance with the evidence and reason; he must give grounds and warrants for his interpretations based on an open analysis of the texts of scripture and tradition. Thus his interpretation is in *principle* refutable by other arguments on the same ground. As Father Lonergan has said, nothing with regard to scripture or tradition is presupposed as an absolute authority today: all that was utterly authoritative before has become "data" for us, to be weighed, interpreted, and affirmed as rational judgment requires, and for no other reason. To appeal to "faith" or "obedience" may in fact be to appeal to traditional interpretations even more at variance with the data and thus detrimental, not conducive, to the discovery of truth.

Secondly, these symbols must be exhibited by the theologian as interpretative of the relevant *ordinary*, "natural" experience of men and women. We must show that their ordinary human experience requires such interpretation to be made coherent and healing, and that these Christian symbols provide the most adequate and coherent interpretation of that natural experience. Only in this way can the traditional symbols be given meaning for us and gain assent from us. The supernatural and the natural are here again not two different realms; rather, supernatural symbols are forms that thematize the natural; symbolic structures that make coherent, intelligible, and meaningful the stuff of natural life. But this process of relating revealed symbols and natural experience requires objective argument: that experience has *this* shape and *this* dimension, that other interpretations are inadequate, and that the Chrisitan symbols interpret our being in the world more adequately and coherently than do others. Such arguments are objective and rational in form; they deal with evidence that can be commonly shared, and they appeal to principles available to any person. In principle, theology, even "existential" theology, should in this way be meaningful and potentially valid to anyone willing to look openly at his own experience and to ponder its implications.

Finally, Christian faith claims to be true, and to have as its object the truth as far as that is possible for human beings. Therefore, since truth is one, because God is one, our theological affirmations must be coherent with all else we believe to be true. And every theology must exhibit this coherence, in principle if not in fact. Among other things this requires that what theology affirms must be shown to be coherent with what scientific inquires state about the world, society, and history. For we do believe in "science" if we ride in elevators, visit our analyst, or call on the sociologist to find out what is going on in the church. Such mediation between theology and science requires philosophy, just as the rendering of theological symbols into concepts and doctrines requires philosophy. So once more we find ourselves appealing to reason, in this case speculative reason, in order to achieve theological understanding and assent.

The use of rational argument based on the widest range of relevant evidence is essential to the theological task at every stage: in achieving fidelity to the traditional symbols, in delineating the meaning of these symbols in ordinary, natural experience, and in relating them to the whole range of truths otherwise known and acknowledged. These objective elements, which convince us that this *is* the most valid understanding of our tradition, that through these symbols natural experience can be made more intelligible and coherent, and that this is the best way to unify the wide variety of truths, are or can be crucial to our personal assent at every stage. Only on such a ground can one affirm Christian faith to be the truth *for me*, and so can assent arise. It almost seems as if St. Voltaire and the Holy Spirit *were* one and the same.

Human understanding, however, is dialectical in character. The grammar of assent contains subjective, involved elements as well as objective ones, and these too must interpenetrate with rational aruments leading to reflective judgments, in theology as in all thought, at every stage or level. One of the most incisive interpreters of scientific thought, Michael Polanyi, has shown that we experience and deeply know much more than we can say or explicate clearly, for example, how to read a map or to ride a bike. And thus we hold as certain by a kind of "tacit understanding" much more than we can demonstrate or prove. This is as true of scientific knowing as it is of common sense knowledge: the criteria, the fundamental paradigms or models, and the norms and purposes of science are not proved but "believed in" by an involved participation and commitment; for they in turn are the basis of all proof. All creative thought is thus "theory-laden," guided by fundamental intuitions about reality and its relation to our thought, and assented to because that thought conforms to the criteria to which we are deeply committed. There is no thought—scientific, philosophical or theological—that is not preceded and upheld by a "stance," a fundamental view of the world and its intelligibility, a view in which we participate through our whole being, and which is historically embodied in some community and borne by a tradition and its fundamental symbols. Participation and involvement are as much elements of our assent to truth as is argument. Thus while argument is always necessary, it is rarely sufficient when we are dealing with the ultimate presuppositions of any field of inquiry.

This interpenetration of rationality and existence, objective and subjective elements, reason and faith, is especially characteristic of religious understanding. For religious symbols, like all fundamental or horizonal symbols, have a *double* reference; they are multivalent in form. They refer to a finite reality on the one hand—the world, history, Israel, Jesus, the church, the goal of history—but on the other they also refer to the transcendent, to the activity of *God* within or in relation to that finite reality. Correspondingly, their truth content *qua* religious symbols is involved in *both* these referents. They communicate truth to us, and we assent to them, only insofar as they speak to us of the transcendent as well as of the finite. Unless we are grasped by the divine expressed in a religious symbol, we do not experience that symbol as "true." Nothing is so devoid of truth content as a religious symbol that has no longer any transcendent referent, as with the gods of a vanished religion. Then the religious symbol in our eyes merely provides false information about the finite, or about an unreal "place" behind the finite, or at best it portrays in pictorial form our own imaginative interpretation of our experience. Religious symbols devoid of religious participation thus become either someone else's superstition or our own art; but in neither case are they vehicles of an assertion about the way things are.

This dependence on participation in religious symbols holds, furthermore, almost as much for their meaning as for their validity. A radically secular mind understands and explains religious symbols (their *real* meaning, as he would put it), not as vehicles of the transcendent but as functions of other finite causes, psychological, social, economic, or political. "Original sin" is a sorry symbol indeed, whose "real meaning" is to be understood in terms of a humanistic hermeneutic of masochism, alienation, or oppression, unless it communicates the real condition of my present humanity and that of my fellows. The meaning of the symbol "original sin" is not understood, nor can it be known to be "true," merely through rational comparison with other symbols on the same level. It is understood as a *religious* symbol (and not as a function merely of psychological or social issues) only when it potentially forms or structures our *own* self-understanding and is seen potentially to lead to the inward experience of repentance and humility; and it can do that only when through it our own relation to the transcendent in some form is made real. In this sense, because of this essential reference to the transcendent, ultimate, or sacred as an intrinsic aspect of its meaning and its truth, it is a *religious* as well as *conceptual* symbol. Thus neither the meaning nor the truth of religious symbols can be found except by a mind open to the transcendent as a dimension of reality. But openness to the transcendent is more a matter of existence, of fundamental stance, than it is of argument, for such a stance determines the kind of arguments and explanations we find relevant and illuminating. On the most fundamental level, religious understanding depends more on an awareness of and participation in the dimension of the transcendent than it does on argument, though argument may help to lead our existence to that awareness and participation.

When, moreover, one moves from the understanding of religious symbols in general to the question of the validity or truth of *certain* religious symbols, and of *this* tradition over against *that* tradition, of a Christian interpretation of our being in the world as opposed to other interpretations, then existential, involved, participatory elements increase. Again arguments are relevant and helpful, and necessary if Christian symbols are to have meaning and to be true for us. Arguments can show that these symbols illumine experience and make it more intelligible than others, and that they provide a more coherent unity of all of experience and its many truths. But our final assent to these symbols appears, when through them the ultimacy that undergirds our lives communicates itself to us. In this experience of illumination, intelligibility, coherence, self-understanding, healing, and hope, we experience the *validity* of the symbols through which that communication has come to us.

This is not to say, therefore, that we must *first* believe or "have faith" in order *then* to understand and to assent to Christian symbols, nor that *what* we believe is by faith presented objective, whole and entire to our judgment for its assent and to our reflection for its theological elaboration. Rather my point is that the deep personal experience of an inner self-understanding, illumination, healing, and confidence *through* these symbols *is* the experience of assent to their meaningfulness and validity, and so is the experience of the beginnings of faith. For what is happening here is that the transcendent—God—is communicating himself to us in and through these symbols: we are grasped, we respond, and faith is born. Argument is relevant: it opens our minds, directs our attention, informs and structures our experience. Argument can lead our own autonomy in the direction of this opening to the transcendent; it can confirm and reconfirm its place there; and it can hold us in that openness. We are led to these symbols, and we listen through them, not only by means of personal, social, and historical crises and their resolution, but also by means of argument. But the symbol is finally *true* for us, and we assent, when through it the transcendent enters our being, grounds, judges, and heals it. God is a meaningful and true object of our thought when he is also the active subject of our thinking, understanding, and our judgment, and so of our reception of the symbol.

Without some participation in the divine, even "natural" argument and important speech themselves tend to wither and die. There must be a participating apprehension of the divine *coherence*, the Logos, for speculative thought to move beyond the immediately given; and thus speculative or metaphysical reason is *itself* a participation in and awareness of the divine as order. There must be participatory confidence in the divine *mystery* so that it does not overwhelm and terrify us, or appear to us as empty, and thought retreat only to what lies immediately before us and so cease to think important thoughts. There must be participation in the divine *mercy* for the uncomfortable truth about ourselves, our history, and our destiny to be known and affirmed without despair. Reason is necessary to theological understanding. But as the above shows, reason can rise to ultimacy in the face of disorder, mystery, and ambiguity, only if ultimacy has first given itself to us for our participation, transformation, confidence, and hope.

Thus the theme of the Holy Spirit enters again into our

talk about assent. Not that we must have faith *before* we understand; nor that it is only in an ecclesiastical sermon that we hear the Word; nor that we must accede in utter obedience to what the church has traditionally said in order to understand our Christian symbols. Rather, our minds can understand the *meaning* of the symbols of our tradition, acknowledge the arguments creative of those meanings, and assent to the arguments assertive of their validity, only when through those symbols we ourselves participate in the transcendent and the divine ground of our being, when through them at last we know ourselves and our destiny aright.

The Catholic tradition has been quite right (against the orthodox and fideist wing of my own tradition, though not against its liberal wing) to emphasize *both* the rational, philosophical elements of theology and the elements of revelation, tradition, authority, and faith. Or, to continue our usage, to welcome both St. Voltaire and the Holy Spirit into the bosom of the *ecclesia*. But the tradition has been wrong wherever these two poles of theological understanding have been separated into two distinct compartments, one of objective secular philosophy based on purely rational argument, and the other of dogmatic theology based on the obedience of faith to tradition and to church authority. Then the theonomous unity of our human being, founded on its existential relation to ultimacy and yet creatively autonomous in rational inquiry and understanding, is split apart into a rational autonomy expressed in philosophy and a religious heteronomy expressed in theology, into a freedom of thought without roots and a unity of religious affirmation untouched by rational criticism or relevant rational elaboration. In such a dichotomy, then, rational argument and disputes, intelligible differences of opinion, and changes of viewpoint are welcomed only with regard to the *preliminary* issues of philosophical inquiry. In the area of *ultimate concern*, with which doctrinal theology deals, obedience to given authority is required, rational debate and disagreement must in the end be silent, and every new and variant viewpoint is suspect. Such an ecclesiastical division into autonomous, rational philosophy and heteronomous, dogmatic theology is, ironically, the mirror image of the spiritual estrangement of our secular culture: on the one side an autonomous intellect ungrounded in ultimate being, truth, and value, and thus in the end unable to deal rationally and creatively with the important issues of life; and on the other an empty and vapid religiosity unrelated to the experience, autonomy, critical freedom, and personal inwardness of contemporary men and women.

In theological understanding, as in creative culture, an interpenetration of the ultimate and the proximate, religious participation and rational inquiry, commitment and rational distance, must take place. At every step of the theological enterprise a dialectic interpenetration of rational argument and involved participation is at work. On the one hand, it is *reason* through its arguments appealing to universally available evidence and acknowledged canons of thought that holds our autonomy fast to the transcendent in the only way it *can* be held, namely freely, by holding itself. On the other hand, it is through participation and involvement that we are related to the transcendent dimension that grounds and upholds our autonomy. Together rational understanding and participatory involvement open us to the transcendent dimension; together they give meaning to our most crucial symbols; and together they create the assent with which we believe, think, and act. There is no Christian understanding (philosophical or otherwise) of our world, of our being within it, our history, and destiny—or of the God who grounds and saves all—without both these dialectical elements. All thinking has some existential root; all religious thought rises *with* a religious existence; and all faith must be understood and found to be persuasive to the mind if it is to be faith. There can be no ultimate and final dichotomy in Christian thinking between philosophy and theology. In theology all statements of faith must be penetrated by autonomous rational criticism, grounding, and elaboration; in turn all rational explication arises from and expresses an ultimate concern for and confidence in the divine coherence and mystery.

My last observations have opened up delicate issues, possibly hidden until now in the somewhat technical discussion of method. These concern the issue of the autonomy (or freedom) and the universality of philosophical judgment on the one hand, and the issues of ecclesiastical authority, dogma, and infallibility, and of the role of theology in the church on the other. For *if* it is true that in creative theological understanding faith and its obedience to the authority of revelation and of the church is *essentially* joined to reason with its criticism of the data, its arguments based autonomously on rational warrants alone, its consequent free judgments, and so its inevitably relative viewpoints, *then* all sorts of questions impinge on us. For now modernity, with its autonomous freedom, relativity of perspectives, and merely probable hypotheses, has entered the sanctum of theology itself, and has affected if not tainted all statements of the church's faith. And if this is the case, then it seems that theology is itself undermined, since it has classically been the task of theology to state that faith in unity and obedience, "that which has been held everywhere and at all times." How, then, is theology so understood as autonomous, relative, and hypothetical related to the transcendent authority of revelation? How is it related to the concrete authority of the church? And finally, how can the church's unity—surely a gift of the Holy Spirit—support or even tolerate a theology so intrinsically wedded to autonomy and its varying, even shifting, perspectives? Can theology be "rational" as modernity is rational? But can theology be "understanding" if it is not rational? For how can the church—even if she be one in dogmatic affirmation—be a community of *belief* and *commitment* unless there is sound understanding and inward assent, founded on reason and its warrants, to the meaning and truth of its symbols?

This dilemma for a modern rationality at work within the Christian tradition is the reflection in intellectual matters of the whole present crisis of Catholicism, as it has been also for two centuries of Protestantism. This crisis can in neither case be resolved by separating the modern reason that lives and works in all of us from the dogmatic affirmations that we as Christians wish to make. They must interpenetrate at every level from foundations, through dogma and doctrines, to praxis, lest our rationality be rootless and our faith be empty, and the whole synthesis of life disintegrate.

Karl Rahner has said that fundamental religious symbols—dogmas, if you please—do not have meaning by themselves. Rather, they mean something to us and gain our real assent and participation only if they are related to our contemporary experience and expressed in our contemporary categories or thought forms. Thus theology must continually reinterpret its most fundamental symbols, re-expressing them ever anew in terms of the changing experience and the changing categories of each age and place. Only in this way can theology be creative, but at the same it is also a *risk*.

I would like to underscore this point and to draw out to the full its implications, though Father Rahner may not see all that I see in his remarks. Theological understanding, as we have analyzed it, is essentially and inescapably *creative*. Its conclusions or doctrinal expressions are not already "given" but are forged by the theologian out of all the materials he has before him in union with his own intuitions about his data and their meanings, his insight into the character of modernity, his personal involvement in the symbols, and his rational ability to think systematically and coherently. A constructive theology—and without *that*, as Rahner says, there is no theology—must first of all draw from scripture and tradition its fundamental symbols and re-express eidetically the given meaning of these symbols. In this hermeneutical process the theologian must *select* the symbols that are to be basic or central and those that are peripheral or irrelevant; for no theology can be built around *all* the symbols of a given tradition. And out of immense and diverse materials he must arrive at one coherent, eidetic meaning for each important symbol. Nothing here is "given" in its final forms; no one can tell him what these symbols (creation, fall, revelation, and so forth) mean or are to mean for his work of synthesis, or even which ones to use centrally. He (or someone else in the distant past) must do this, or it is not done at all. This task involves both creative thought on the biblical and historical materials, and personal participation. For he selects according to relevance and truth for him and for his time, and so in that process both rational judgment and personal involvement are required. His obedience *guides* his free and creative thought; it cannot coerce it into prior conclusions, lest he end up again with Denzinger.

Similarly, when he relates these symbols to contemporary experience, and rethinks them in terms of contemporary ontology (and in so doing transforms both the ontology in which they were once set *and* the ontology he has borrowed from contemporary philosophers) he is perforce creative, thinking out their meaningfulness and conceptuality *anew*. What he achieves is thus again a risk, different from the old, and deviant in important ways from the orthodox and traditional meanings; else it is not relevant to its time, nor is it theology or understanding. In this way his theological thought, like all thought, is historical, rooted in his own time and place; it must be so rooted to be relevant, to be *religious*, personally meaningful, and true to him and to us who are also of that time and place. But by the same token it is new, different, creative, a novel perspective on Christian truth, different from the interpretations of the past, different from the interpretations in Asia or Africa, and different, alas, from the interpretations in Rome!

If all thought is thus *historical*, and if the object of theological understanding is a mystery never fully expressed or expressible by any of us, then let us note that total *unity* of thought in the church is in fact more restrictive than is variety, both over time and space. For a total unity of human thought means conformity to *one* finite and limited perspective! Correspondingly, variety in principle means the transcendence of that partial conformity. The church is thus more inclusive, more universal, more *catholic* when it embodies over time and space a variety of viewpoints than when it holds rigidly to one partial one. Granting the finitude, the historicity of our perspectives, ecumenicity, and variety of viewpoints are the sole means to catholicity. None of us as theologians has *the* truth, and no theology we or anyone else creates embodies *the* truth. Each of our reflective proposals becomes *theology* when it is new, and creative—a risk. We all *intend* the truth, and that intention is our obedience and fidelity, but we are inescapably historical, and undeniably our calling is to be creative. Thus while what we all intend in theology is universal, what we in fact achieve and express in understanding—in philosophy or theology—is partial. The Holy Spirit, therefore, is *more* alive in the church when a singleness of intention results in a plurality of creative viewpoints.

I wish now to draw out one more important implication of all this, namely its implication for the relation of theology to the authority of the church, especially to the *magisterium*. The reason I presume to speak of this is that to me the issue is important because, despite some increasingly secondary points of bafflement and even criticism which I acknowledge in myself with regard to Catholic theory and practice, I regard the resolution of Catholicism's most significant dilemmas as the most important thing that can happen for the whole church in the present. If Christianity is to survive and be vital, that is, authentic, it will only be because Catholicism has survived and become authentic. If Catholicism is to prosper creatively, it is essential that she reinterpret her own institutional structures and reshape them into forms appropriate and meaningful to modernity and powerful in our time—much as theology must reinterpret and reshape its symbols. This is also a creative and risky task, to uncover what a twentieth-century institutional form of *Catholicism* is and can be; and it requires the most fundamental criticism, creative rethinking, and practical work on every basic structure of that institution.

The historicity and partiality of any theological viewpoint means that the task of theology cannot be understood normatively as that of "stating the faith of the church." If there is in fact such variety of perspective, and if his view is to be genuinely creative, the theologian could not possibly, try as he might, accomplish that task. In dealing with fundamental matters—and there is no *theology* if such matters are not also rethought—no one can possibly state "the faith" to everyone's satisfaction in his own time and place, nor *a fortiori* can anyone even dream of representing in his own theology what "has everywhere and at all times been held to be true"! And heaven help the theologian and his church if he is judged and declared out of court by only one partial viewpoint when he seeks to state a creative and new interpretation.

A recurrent dilemma arises here. If a theologian is to be

understood and judged in terms of the criterion that he must satisfactorily "state the faith of the whole church," then *either* other theologians must agree with this new viewpoint as in fact "*the* faith of the church" and become thereby his disciples, or else they must call him a heretic, out of court for enunciating a "non-Catholic" position. Or perhaps worst of all, as the consequence of this impossible dilemma between universal discipleship and heresy, the theologian more and more deals only with unimportant issues on which disagreement is legitimate because it does not touch the Catholic core of faith and so does not threaten unity on essential matters. In the latter case, theology curls up and dies—and in the end the church with it. For fundamental issues *above all* must be reviewed, reconceived, and re-expressed if theology is to be relevant and if religious assent is to be possible in our age.

If plurality of viewpoint, even on fundamental matters, is built into the historical character of the church, then we can only welcome in the name of the Holy Spirit an alternative view that we *do not* share. Such a view with which we disagree is, of course, precisely one which we do *not* think states adequately "the faith of the church" (which is, presumably, why we do not share it). How else besides the possibility of diversity and disagreement on fundamental matters are creativity and relevance *possible* in a human community of whose perspectives all are partial? Are not variety and disagreement on fundamentals necessary if the confinement of our common thought to one partial interpretation is to be transcended, as everyone agrees it must be? Most of us are considered to be heretics by a good many Christians. And what is heresy to me is and always has been the strange and often repudiated parent of good theology in the church as a whole.

Thus in the name of the Holy Spirit, and of the possibilities both of a Catholic theology and of a creative relevant theology, let us say with Voltaire: "I do not agree with what you say, but I will fight to the death for your right to say it." In this strange and deep way the Holy Spirit and Voltaire *are* one: out of a plurality of discussion, grounded by the Spirit at work in the community, the faith of the church will issue in valid expression.

Since all theologians are partial, historical men and all have as their task the creative reinterpretation of the symbols of our faith, and since all speak as best they can of a mystery that ever transcends our partial speech, no one theologian can state *the* faith of the church. We can *intend* it to be sure. But all that we do and can do in actuality is to offer a *proposal* to the wider community, that in our time the faith and its symbols can be understood in *this* way; a proposal we hope will be discussed, transformed, rejected, or accepted by the community in its thought and life. And we can only have confidence that through the work of the Spirit—and the enthusiastic criticism of our colleagues—this proposal will be cleansed and purified and thus made a more fitting vehicle of Christian understanding.

But what if it is wrong? It *will* be wrong; partial, incomplete, and wayward. None of us can be justified by our work or our obedience; and certainly no theologian can proceed confident that *he* has at last found the truth of either the faith or the church. We are justified by our faith alone—in this case by our faith in the Holy Spirit and its intrinsic and indissoluble relation to the community of the church and the development of its thought. To believe in the Holy Spirit as at work in the church preserving there the truth of the faith is to believe that out of the reflection and the criticisms of the whole community the truth will be both preserved *and* refashioned; that, as in all the church's history, present as well as past, out of the wayward variety of human creativity and error, God will work wonders.

# Chapter VII

## *Addressing God in Faith*

IN THIS CONCLUDING chapter I want to discuss the most fundamental way in which what we call "the contemporary crisis of faith" manifests itself: the elusiveness in our time of the *holy*, the absence for countless persons of a vivid sense of the presence of the divine—an absence felt not only in daily life in the world but (even more devastating) an absence brought from the world into holy places and experienced when Christians gather together in worship. This absence of deity in our common worship contributes to and even founds our other religious and theological problems. Were the presence of God real for us at least in worship, contemporary problems of belief or of God-language would be minimal, matters only of translation into current worldly modes of validation and of common, ordinary forms of discourse. That, on the contrary, questions of the possibility of belief and of the meaningfulness of language about God are deep and significant issues even for the worshipping community indicates, therefore, that at the heart of that community's life, in its common worship, a compelling absence is experienced. For affirmation in faith of the reality of God and discourse about him alike depend upon an experience of his living presence. Thus the reality of common worship is the center on which both Christian religious existence and theology depend. We cannot evoke that reality by theological reflection—for, as with proofs of God, the dependency runs the other way—but in such reflection we know that we move not toward the periphery of our ultimate concerns in theology but closer to their source and ground.

If there are problems in Christian worship peculiar to our age as well as those common to all periods, these former problems stem from the cultural or historical world that permeates us and that we bring with us into church. More of modernity than loud speakers, sophisticated lighting, and air conditioning inhabits our places of worship: the people who listen, kneel, and search for the divine presence in Word and Sacrament are also "modern," suffused with a secular consciousness that has tended to dissolve the sense of the holy wherever that consciousness has become dominant. Thus the words they hear communicate to them more about their clerical leader and his notions than about the divine Word; the elements they receive are for many, if not most, merely signs of traditional sacralities, not living symbols of the divine presence; and the experiences they enjoy are for them at best their own subjective reactions and not the workings of the Holy Spirit.[1] The holy has appeared in the history of Christian worship in a variety of forms as sacrament, as Word, as spiritual possession. In each case the holy has not appeared alone or directly, but through the medium of something earthly—elements, speech, and feelings. Now, even though the cultural reasons for its contemporary absence from these traditional media of the holy may not be consciously known or reflectively pondered (for example, a historical view of all words, even sacred ones, or a psychological view of all inner experi-

ences), still the absence of the transcendent in and
through these media is universally *felt*—and thus our
worship is a problem.

For worship is not a self-generated activity; it is rather
a response to the presence of the holy objectively experienced in our midst. It is not something that can be created
or even evoked by us. As in revelation, it is *there* within
its medium to be responded to (and that response is worship), or it is not there at all; hence if it is not there
objectively for us, there can be no worship as response to
its presence. Consequently, as every liturgist, traditional
or experimental, knows, it is impossible to "create a sense
of worship" by changing bodily movements, words, lights,
or music; nor by merely refashioning our forms of worship
can we "make worship real." It may well be important for
the possibility of our human response that such changes
in liturgy be made. But the prior and more fundamental
problem of the presence of the holy is another matter, for
neither the repetition of traditional usages nor the adop-
tion of new ones will in itself bring about *that* presence.[2]
All *we* can do is to free our forms and to increase their
relevance so that they can communicate the holy to us. It
is God's presence that evokes worship, not our act of worship that brings forth God.

Thus reflection on the problem of worship, insofar as it
can be of help at all, is driven in the first instance not so
much to consider more appropriate forms of worship as to
reconsider and reappropriate the modes of presence of the
holy in our tradition, to ponder at its deepest level how
God comes to us in our community and our faith, to explore the most fundamental question of theology: how is
God related to man, and how does man's awareness of
that divine presence arise and flourish? The history of
worship, of piety, and of theology are therefore distinct
but not separate histories; each history in its own way
reflects the varying modes of the divine presence. When-

ever worship has been vital and strong, its forms, as well as those of piety and theology, have been shaped by some vivid mode of the divine presence—as, for example, Reformation worship reflected the same manifestation of the holy through the Word that was also the center both of Reformation religious life and of its theology. Consideration of worship at the most fundamental level, then, is consideration of the presence of God to men. It involves every basic theological doctrine concerning the activity of God on us, in us, and on our world. By pondering the mystery of the presence of God in our being and living, we may be able to open our minds and ourselves to more special and concentrated forms of awareness of that presence—for worship is the community together celebrating and responding to that presence. In the following, therefore, we shall try to think out the character of Christian worship at this fundamental level in the light of our theological understanding of the presence of God in human experience.

How is the holy experienced in Christian existence? Or, put more objectively, how does God relate himself to man in Christian faith? This dual question, as I have noted earlier, may well form the most fundamental question in theology; it surely does when we try to think out the theological foundations for worship. We shall here consider this question both formally and materially, with regard to the forms of our experience of the holy, and with regard to its matter, or more specifically, to the levels of our life in which this experience manifests itself. Such an examination may relate again the modes of Christian worship to our real experiences of sacrality—and thus, in reminding us of the continual presence of the holy in our existence, open us to its concentrated presence in communal worship.

We do not experience God directly in this life.[3] We are immersed in the creaturely and historical world God has created, and if we are aware of his presence at all, it is in and through his activity in that world, in and through what we call nature, history and its events, and our fellowmen and ourselves. The presence of God is always in a manner "hidden," hidden within a finite medium that at once maintains its own creaturely integrity, powers, possibilities, and weaknesses, and yet manifests within itself the presence and activity of the divine. This fundamental pattern of divine presence within the creaturely is most universally expressed in the notion of creation: each entity is and continues to be in its integrity and autonomy because of the divine activity in it of creation and preservation. It is further expressed in the doctrine of providence: the patterns of historical change brought about by creaturely action manifest as well the activity and the purposes of God.

But this "sacramental" or "theonomous" principle reaches its strongest and clearest expression in the incarnation: the presence of God for Christian faith is pradigmatically seen in the fully human person of Jesus. In each case the sacred or divine is present in and through the finite; in turn the finite in becoming fully itself is a vehicle or medium for that inward grace. For the creature to understand itself and its destiny *truly* as finite, and therefore to achieve its own true or "natural" integrity and autonomy, is to understand itself in that way, namely as upheld, directed, called, and healed by the divine power. In this sense one can say that nature in its true being is not separated from grace. On the contrary, each creature is naturally a symbol, in the *first* sense of that word, of the presence of the holy, and it becomes its authentic self when the pattern of its life inwardly and outwardly reflects that created status and role.[4] But this divine presence, and the role or status of the creature as symbol, is hidden within the integrity of finitude itself and veiled by our alienation from the sacred source and ground of our life. This presence must be reawakened and reappropriated in all of us by special manifestations of the sacred; as a race and as individuals we must be "twice-born" because we are separated by our common sin from our own essential natures and so from an awareness of and a life within that continuing divine presence. It is in these particular manifestations of the sacred that the different religious traditions find their religious or theological (as opposed to their historical or cultural) roots and differentia. Here arises, then, a *second* sense of the word symbol, namely those special and unique media through which a particular revelation of the ultimate and the sacred (universally present but also universally obscured) is now manifested in a particular form to a historical community, and through which that group becomes aware of its own status as symbol (in the first sense), as existing in and through the power of the divine. In our Christian tradition, the significant symbols in this second sense are the history of the community of Israel and the person of Jesus.

Finally, in each tradition this presence of the divine in and through special events and persons is communicated over time to the community founded upon that special presence. This communication is in turn achieved through "symbols" in a *third* sense of that word. Again, finite entities have become media that point to, recall, and reintroduce by representation the originating presence of the holy in the symbols creative of that tradition. Such tertiary symbols are infinitely various in religion; in our tradition they are most importantly composed of communal acts and elements (sacraments) on the one hand, and spoken and reflected words on the other (*kerygma, didache* and the theological symbols that further reflection draws from them, such as creation, providence, incarnation, atonement, eschatological promises, and so forth). Both sacrament and word are essential if our theological understanding of the divine presence is correct.

Ultimacy is present in our living and being human, in the totality of our existence, not just to our minds and consciences. This *ontological* presence of the holy can be brought to awareness and recommunicated to us only through media that are as we are, and that analogically also communicate our being to us, such as water, bread, and wine. On the other hand, the presence of the holy is hidden in the finite—in ourselves and in these special media. Its presence must be evoked for us by a word that penetrates through the creaturely vehicle to the transcendent that appears within it and so a word that brings that transcendent dimension to our personal awareness— whether it be the transcendent at work in a historical event, in a sacramental element, or in our own existence.[5] Sacrament and Word, ontological presence and *kerygma*, are essentially and yet dialectically interrelated in communicating the divine presence; this dialectical interrelation of the ontological and the personal or reflective levels will deepen as we proceed.

In turn our awareness of and response to the presence of the sacred, which is the heart of the problem of worship as response to the holy, combines these three senses of the word "symbol." All Christian worship points to and finds its center in the symbols originative of that tradition, to the Word in covenant and prophecy and the Word made flesh. Correspondingly, the role of the tertiary symbols is to accomplish that pointing and centering. The sacraments of baptism and eucharist with all of their manifold symbolic power re-present to us these originating events, and the *kerygma* or proclamation opens up to us the transcendent meaning of those events and calls us to decision and commitment in relation to them. As I pointed out in earlier chapters, the classical forms of Christian worship, Catholic and Protestant, have emphasized—and often overemphasized to the exclusion of the other—one or the other of these two forms of tertiary symbol. Certainly a more inclusive reinterpretation of both media is essential to the renewal of each of these two forms of Christian communion.

I suspect, however, that the present weakness of both classical forms of Christian worship lies not so much in this overemphasis as in their common indifference to the first meaning of "symbol" as we delineated it, i.e., that the divine works in and on *us* as creatures too, and that awareness of *our* role as symbols—in our being, meaning, decisions, and hopes—lies at the heart of any experience of the holy that is to be relevant to and effective in us. Put in terms of the history of ecclesiology, this may be called a plea for a renewed "spiritualist" principle in worship in which the relation in awareness of worshipper to God is primary; or in terms of contemporary philosophy, a plea for an "existential" relation on our part to sacrament and Word alike. In terms of our previous theological discussion, our argument is that unless the symbols of our tradition in Word and sacrament are brought into relation to the ultimacy that permeates our ordinary life, unless traditional symbols reawaken in us our role as symbols of the divine activity—there is no experience of the holy.

Sacramental and kerygmatic symbols remain meaningless and ineffective unless they communicate the holy to us, and that means unless they bring to our awareness the presence of the holy throughout the total character of our own existence. Thus in a secular age when ordinary life is separated in its self-understanding from its own transcendent ground, sacramental symbols unrelated to the transcendent dimensions of our own existence in life become magical or merely traditional, and kerygmatic symbols change into empty theologisms or anachronistic signs of our moral and intellectual autonomy. The worship that responds to the Christian presentation of the holy in Word and sacrament must be so related to lived experience that these traditional symbols communicate to us an awareness of our own essential relation to the holy. In order to be alive, religious symbols must provide shape to the patterns of ordinary life; correspondingly, natural, "secular" life must receive its fundamental forms from these symbols if it is to achieve its own essential goodness. God is already there in our existence as its ultimate ground and its ultimate goal. The role of sacrament and Word alike is not so much to create or insert that presence into nature but to bring forth that prior relation in awareness and to give it the shape, power, and form of Jesus Christ. The clue to renewed worship, as of a renewed Christian existence and theology, insofar as by reflection we can take hold of these matters, is to reappropriate through the forms of Christian symbolism the presence of the holy in the totality of ordinary existence.

If the goal of worship is to reawaken through concentrated expression (an expression formed by Jesus Christ) our awareness of the ultimacy that grounds and permeates our entire existence, then possibly our next question concerns the ways the holy manifests itself in our existence—how it is that we too are "symbols" of the presence of the divine activity.[6] For relevant, meaningful, and effective modes of worship will be those that, besides being faithfully Christian, bring to awareness the modes of our own participation in and relation to the holy. Our discussion of the modes of manifestation of the holy in the totality of our existence may well in addition provide insight into both the perennial questions concerning our understanding of God and the perennial problems about the interrelation in worship of the ontological and the moral, the impersonal and the personal.

If God, as Christians believe, is the source and ground of our whole being, then the holy is crucially present on every level of our existence, providing the basis for every one of our essential or ontological powers. This active presence of ultimacy, giving our human nature its possibility and its form, may not be an aspect of our direct awareness, though, as we have argued elsewhere,[7] we all have as humans a subliminal awareness of the ultimate dimension in which we live. Still, this *is* the way we are related to God, and thus any sense in worship of the presence of God, while evoked for us by the symbols of our specific Christian tradition, will also be in part formed by the ways God works in and through us in our ordinary being and living.

There are many levels to our existence, and there are innumerable ways in which these different levels can be discriminated and named. Basic to all is the level of our being as such, our existence and life. Contingent, partial, and transitory as it is, our finite being is the ground of all our activities and values, and thus on every score of ultimate concern to us. We experience ultimacy initially in relation to the question of our being and our nonbeing as contingent creatures; thus an awareness of the holy is, or can be, communicated to us through our celebration of the gift of our own being. Through apprehension of the creation of our contingent being, we can be personally aware of the lived meaning of the symbol of creation—and thus of the presence of the holy on that ontological level.

Secondly, fundamental to our sense of worth or meaning in what we are and do is a context of ultimate meanings within which we act. This ultimate context of relations, social and historical, spanning past, present, and future, is as necessary to our human being as is our existence. Awareness of this context as expressive of the divine ultimacy is therefore a second way of apprehending the holy as it manifests itself to us, a manifestation expressed symbolically in God's providential judgment and care over us and our history.

Again, when as rational beings we seek to understand and to know ourselves and our world, we also encounter ultimacy and sacrality under the form of truth.[8] In apprehending this ultimacy in our ordinary existence, we may be able to apprehend the presence of the holy in worship under the Christian symbols of the divine Logos and the divine truth.

As autonomous beings we encounter the sacred as moral norm and so as obligation and responsibility, probably our first and most direct touch with deity in our developing experience. Following on this experience of the sacred as norm, the holy stands in our fallen existence over against us as condemnation, guilt, and alienation; and we seek for renewal, self-acceptance, and reconciliation. A plethora of Christian symbols correspond to and answer these secular experiences of conscience and judgment and the search for reconciliation that they inspire: law, wrath, and grace.

Finally, we live in time amidst radical change and are thus both energized and haunted by the "new" in the future. Our life, if it is to be human, must have confidence in this "new" that is to come, a new that will characterize both our individual and our social, historical existence. We can only live and act creatively if we have hope, a hope based on some promise for our own future and that of our race. The fundamental eschatological symbols of our faith, based on God's promises for the future, both proximate and ultimate, answer therefore to this basic human drive toward and openness to the future that impinges upon us.

These are all quite ordinary experiences suffusing our daily existence; they stem from and point to ultimacy as it works in and on our being. To bring this ultimacy in its forms alike as existence and meaning, norm, wrath, grace and promise, which is God, to awareness and commitment as it is known in Christ, is to experience "faith"; and to respond to that ultimacy apprehended in and through these Christian symbols and in the form of Jesus Christ is to worship God. Word and sacrament provide the symbols by which this encounter with the holy is shaped and restored; but it is the holy as it founds, permeates, and restores our daily being that gives life, reality, and meaning to these symbols and that provides the *presence* to which we respond in worship.

Essential to this view is the affirmation of a parallel or correlation, as well as a crucial distinction, between the workings of the holy in and on us in our daily secular life and the deeper meanings of the Christian symbols or doctrines—and so between general and special revelation, nature and grace, God as creative providence and God as redeemer. Thus the symbols (in senses two and three) of our faith manifest to us our own status and role as by nature symbols (in sense one) or "creatures." And thus our ordinary experience, apprehended in its ultimate dimension, gives to our Christian worship its life, revelance, and power.

Also essential to this view is the affirmation that while grace in and through Jesus Christ (what we have called a secondary level of symbol) brings something radically new and utterly unmerited into our ordinary existence, it does so only because of our fallen state, our separation from God and from our own natures in the exclusively autonomous rather than theonomous character of our existence. It is not to make up for a lack in our created nature that the unmerited and surprising grace communicated to us by the special revelation in Jesus Christ comes to us, but to overcome the distortion we have made in our natures and in our history. Redemption fulfills creation; it does not transform it into something else or even something higher, as if to fulfill our created human natures were not a high enough goal for a human existence, and as if that human goal did not have its own genuine glory in being at one and the same time a creative creature and also a symbol of the divine activity in history. But we must add that in refashioning our human being into its own created structure and purpose as such a symbol, grace also projects us into a *new* future—of ourselves and of history—that itself has a goal far beyond that of a mere repetition or even a restoration of the temporal past. Directedness towards an eschatological goal is the essential nature of both divine and human being, and so again grace in no way transcends nature but rather makes its realization and fulfillment possible.

If this analysis is correct, several conclusions follow about God and our relation in worship to him. The first is the multiplicity of categories involved in God's relation to us; these are ontological and moral, impersonal and personal, a fact that should warn us against an overemphasis on either the ontological or the purely personal in understanding God or in structuring worship (as Catholics and Protestants both tend to do). This plethora of categories appears, so to speak, twice. First, because the holy works in and on us, and thus can manifest itself to us on *all* levels of our existence from the level of our being or existence itself right up to the level of our rational and moral autonomy, i.e., from the impersonal organic base of our life to its personal heights. Secondly, on each of these levels there is a dialectic between an active divine presence that is *there* whether we are personally aware of it or not (expressed, for example, in the symbols of the divine creation, providence, judgment, and care), and our personal apprehension of and response to that presence. An integration of this continual ontological presence of the holy with our own personal apprehension of and response to it is the heart of worship. Thus again our understanding of our relation to God and our participation in that relation in worship span ontological and moral, unconscious and reflective, impersonal and personal categories. God is both in us ontologically as an ultimate power of which we become aware, and over against us as a person whom we encounter in moral obligation and religious commitment, and so whom we can address in dialogue. Neither set of categories can be used exclusively or univocally in theology or in worship. It is no arbitrary accident, then, that full worship—like full theological reflection—includes ontological, intentional, moral, and personal levels, and that in the case of each of these levels, sacramental presence and personal word require each other. Without the element of sacramental presence, a form of worship composed only of reflective and moral concepts (as in liberal Protestantism) omits celebration of the divine ground of our fundamental being and our deepest meanings, the ontological context within which we think and act. Thus it tends to dissipate its religious dimension into a celebration of our personal autonomy. On the other hand, without the continual presence of *word* making possible personal reflection, decision, appropriation, and commitment, the element of sacramental presence fails to reach our personal being and thus tends to be reduced to a mere traditionalism that can border on the rote and even the magical.

A further implication of this understanding of the holy and its presence to us in and through symbols gives the twofold basis for the social or communal character of worship. The secondary and tertiary symbols through which the holy is reawakened and reappropriated (originating revelation and its symbolic witness in sacrament and word) come to us in history through a tradition, that is, through a community structured by these symbols. In this community and through these symbols the holy that permeates our ordinary life has come to our awareness, and in faith our life is now grounded, directed, called, and healed. Thus our own experience and worship of the holy is essentially communal in its origin and its actualization; it is not and cannot be something that we do alone merely as individuals, either in time or in space.

Secondly, man as man is both ontologically and personally communal. Our existence and life, our personal being, the possibility and modes of our speech, reflections, and activities come to us from community and take the forms of our own communal origin. We cannot be as human beings without society. Therefore any apprehension of the ultimate mystery that founds and upholds our human being inevitably culminates in a social apprehension, for it is as fellowmen and not as individuals that we are there as human.

Thirdly, Christian man is social and communal: he celebrates his creation through the life and love of other human beings, and he is called by the gospel to minister to others if he is to be whole. He arises out of love both human and divine, and he is sent forward into love and community as the deepest personal meaning of his human being. On every ground, then, man's relation to the divine is both personal and social; as the ontological and the personal levels interpenetrate in worship at every level, so no individual man or woman, and especially no Christian, can apprehend, celebrate, or obey the holy except in community.

Finally, worship has an historical and ultimately an eschatological *telos* and fundamental meaning. Because we are ontologically and morally communal beings, made from and for each other, and because we exist in time so that what we are is a projection toward an end, therefore the holy in its creative, providential, normative, and redemptive work on us moves us away from ourselves outward into history and forward into the future. This ontological fact about our being receives its fullest symbolic expression in the Kingdom to which we are called in this life and beyond it in eternity, and whose coming is the key to understanding the divine intentionality structuring all we can know of the holy. The divine ultimacy that founds and upholds us in the present, and that calls us out into the social and historical world and forward into that world's future, is itself directed forward to its own divine goal. Our apprehension of God and our response to him, therefore (like our apprehension of and actualization of ourselves and our history), are temporal and eschatological, directed into a future whose mystery remains but whose ultimate shape is to be determined by the same love and power that in our Christian present has already established us.

Let me close this discussion with some remarks about Word and sacrament in the new setting of a worship oriented not toward a special religious sphere—the two-zone view—but as the ground, critic, and inspirer of the secular sphere, the ordinary life-world of man. Since the Enlightenment it has frequently been assumed that with the growth of autonomy, self-consciousness and subjectivity in modern culture, the Protestant principle of the Word addressed to intellect and conscience would slowly displace the anachronistic, materialistic and "magical" Catholic sacramental principle. And there is not a little in recent modern Catholic liturgical reforms (most of which I heartily approve) that might seem to agree: the emphasis on the vernacular, on personal participation by the laity, on biblical sermons, and so forth. I would like to dispute this general view, however, and, unless such a caveat is too paradoxical from a free churchman, to assert in our day the *priority* of the sacramental in Christian liturgy—after stating some of the reasons the Protestant principle of the Word is also important for us all.

The most fundamental reasons for the Word have already been supplied, namely, the principles of the transcendence of deity and of the integrity of the finite. Thus when the divine is either active in the life-world or present in specifically liturgical action, its presence is hidden within the finite media. There are few visible theophanies

in our traditions; thus unless that presence had been proclaimed and interpreted, as is clear in both the prophetic
and the apostolic traditions, it would have remained in-
cognito to those who witnessed the events and to us who
ponder them. Further, it is neither the visible creaturely
medium to which faith is directed, nor the transcendent in
and of itself. Rather faith addresses itself to the two in
dialectical conjunction. It is therefore the Word of witness alone that directs us beyond the medium to the holy
present within it. Without the principle of the Word, the
sacramental principle of presence is in danger of con-
founding the sacred and its medium, and relinquishing,
therefore, both the transcendence and sacrality of deity
and the autonomy and integrity of the creature. This
identification of the finite medium with the sacred transcendent to it has been fatal at every point that it has
appeared in Church history. But it would be especially
fatal in the secular context we envisage if the sacred were
identified with the creaturely symbol as such, with ourselves, our community, and our social world.

Secondly, the Word is necessary as the principle of
judgment on the estranged character of all human life,
even life lived in the presence of deity, where the servants
of God are by their very closeness to deity prone to identify themselves with it. The Word is that in revelation
which manifests the infinite qualitative difference between holy and profane, and thus in judging brings the
only grounds for hope for a reduction of that difference.
Finally, the Word addresses uniquely the inward and
temporal spirit of man; sacramental presence is fundamental to our faith but that presence is both inward and
personal, and so must be spoken, and it is proleptic, a
promise for the future. And neither one—the grace of
judgment, forgiveness, acceptance, and justification, nor
the eschatological promises—can be communicated except by personal word.

Lest this seem, however, to end in a Protestant peroration, let me say that to me the Catholic principle of sacramental presence, taken in its epistemological, ontological, and liturgical scope, is basic to our faith. This is obvious from all I have said. After all, the theory of revelation enunciated here is a sacramental and not a verbal theory of divine manifestation in which the divine presence in a multitude of forms and modes, rather than the "divine speech," is regarded as the ontological and epistemologically prior level of revelation. Incidentally, the essential and prior character of the principle of sacramental presence must be asserted, not only against Protestant theologians of divine speech but presently also against the siren calls of the best Catholic theologians to abandon the divine presence in past and present and to "speak" only of an eschatological presence to come in the future, a theology of the Word alone with a vengeance! All I have said about the divine presence throughout experience indicates that the possibility of meaningful theological speech, and so of the Word itself, depends upon our awareness of that sacramental presence. No God of the future can be promised meaningfully to us, and no future Kingdom can be relevant to what we do politically today, unless there is that presence at work in our common life. Sacramental presence, the divine activity in and through all of creation, precedes and grounds Word and promise alike, as Catholicism preceded and grounded the personal and autonomous forms of Protestantism.

This is, however, not merely a matter of grounding; no great tradition likes to feel like a basement, however essential to the upper floors! My further point is that the character of modern culture to me calls more for a Catholic, sacramental principle of mediation than it does for the Protestant verbal principle—and this is why I emphasize it everywhere. Ours is an age in which all that is historical is relative; thus all speech, words, concepts, propositions, dogmas and laws are to us historically relative, subject to qualification, infinitely human, and therefore contestable. A mediation of the absolute through words, however venerable, is intensely difficult: either the mediating speech must claim to be itself absolute, or it must admit its relativity, i.e., either the priest states authoritative and infallible dogmas, or admits they are merely his own opinions, and neither one is in our day a possible or a happy solution. Ours is also an age fortunately reawakened to the intimacy of the relations of body to spirit, of the spirituality of the bodily and the sensual, if you will. The sensory and the aesthetic are thus for us again, after centuries, possible media of spiritual insight. Again, the Word alone, addressed to intellect and conscience, is inadequate. With sacramental media, on the other hand, we can recognize the finite and relative character of the media and not lose the mediation; "symbol" is a better word than either "dogma" or "doctrine" on this point. Sacramental mediation can relate us to the absolute and unconditioned by means of relative symbols, for the symbol participates in the relativity of the creaturely world from which it arises and yet it communicates an infinity in which it participates. Such mediation, moreover, can relate us to ultimacy through a wide variety of symbolic forms—verbal, conceptual, aesthetic, bodily. A Catholicism that has relinquished its absolutism and has recognized the new world of relativity, and yet that as Catholic and sacramental can still relate grace and the wondrous width of divine activity to the total life-world of men and women, *this* Catholicism may well find itself more relevant to modern needs, more creative in the modern situation, and less anachronistic to modern sensibilities than any form of Protestantism. Strangely, in denying or objuring—or being forced by the twentieth century to do so!—the great *temptation* of a sacramental form of religion to absolutize the relative and sanctify the ambiguous, Catholicism may discover the vast strength of a sacramental form of religion, namely, the divinely granted capacity to allow finite and relative instruments to be media of the divine and to endow all of secular and ordinary life with the possibility and the sanctity of divine creativity; and thus more than Protestantism, Catholicism may be able to bring Christianity alive and well through the turmoil of the modern world.

However, if Catholicism, or Protestantism, is to achieve this task of mediating the divine grounding, judgment, and possibility to our secular existence, it must widen the scope of both Word and sacrament far beyond their present religious, ecclesiastical, dogmatic, and "merely redemptive" limits. If, for example, the Word is to provide through the proclamation and teaching of verbal and notional symbols the basis for all of our existence, our understanding of those symbols must include their relation to the social, public life of man, as well as to his individual virtues and vices, weals and woes. The proclaimed Word must intersect, in judgment and in approbation, in critical analysis and deep support, the whole realm of *social* symbolism we analyzed, a relation of deep and potentially dangerous idolatry on the one hand, but on the other the necessary condition for creative human life, since we humans cannot *be* at all, especially in a divine Kingdom, without a symbolic social structure. As Augustine said, every state strives for ultimate peace and justice, and then fails, establishing at best only a perverted peace and justice, and an incomplete humanity. To refashion our social world into an approximation of the promised Kingdom, and thus to help in the liberation of men and women, is one of the major themes of the gospel and so one of the major tasks of the church catholic. Only in this way can it be creative in a secular world. And a world moving deeper and deeper into a dehumanizing technology, into fundamental shifts of world power, into the new nightmare of scanty resources, will need all the humanizing of its social structures it can get.

Even more needs to be done to widen the scope or range of the sacraments. Ideally the sacramental system of an unfallen church (is such a notion conceivable?) would mediate the divine grace to every facet of natural life, to all the major stages, crises, and points of intense meaning of our ongoing life-world. Thus in a sacramental universe (and sacramentalists like that phrase, though they do not necessarily like the full implications of it), the sacraments would bring to explicit expression at appropriate points the divine presence in all of life, as the divine Word would mediate the divine judgment and mercy to all the issues of common human life. And yet this is not what they do, or even seek to do, at all. Rather in their classical form (and at this deep level are they still not entirely traditional?), they relate the divine presence not to human life generally and in its natural course but only to human beings as they enter *ecclesia*, the covenant community, the special and separate realm of redemption, the churchly realm of grace. Baptism is not at all a sacrament of birth, of the divine gift of being, of life, of human existence, though our faith and creed emphasize the centrality of the divine creation. On the contrary, baptism is solely a sacrament of the forgiveness of sins, and of entrance, not into the *human* but into the *religious* community. What a strange Marcionic vision within a Catholic system that names God "being," and then acts sacramentally as if the gift of being were secular and not worthy of sacramental notice!

Confirmation, the Christian rite of initiation, is not with us a rite of entrance into adulthood and the adult community, a sacrament celebrating, blessing and molding the divine gift of autonomy and responsibility and so of adult and responsible community. Rather, confirmation represents solely the entrance into Mother Church, as if there for the first time we met the divine presence. How strange again that a Catholic system should contest the Enlightenment secularization of autonomy and responsibility, and then reduplicate that very secularization in its sacramental system.

The sacrament of ordination or of orders: here is the blessed sacrament of vocation, of the divine gift of meaningful activity in the world, and for the neighbor, and thus for God and his Kingdom. Do clerics alone do this work in their religious tasks? Does the creative activity of the layman, an activity instrumental in increasing the Kingdom as we now define it, namely, as a social order of liberation, justice, and humanity, then derive not at all from the divine power and purpose?

Theologically and ethically Christians proclaim that the task of the church is that of liberating and humanizing God's world, and we define the eschatological promises in that light. Yet our sacraments fail to point us in this direction, toward the world and its life. A similar analysis could be made of marriage, penance and unction; again each is in principle directed at central issues of human existence but traditionally concerned only with the way those issues appear, or reappear, in the special covenant community of grace. The Eucharist needs no redirecting, for it is the center; but it needs freeing; its scope needs an infinite widening and extension over the whole earth. And this widening could, I suggest, be the special role of the other sacraments, namely, to relate not only (as traditionally) to rebirth but also to birth, not only to life in the *ecclesia* but to life in God's world, and thus to help to mediate the divine presence to all of life as it moves into God's future. And this entrance into the center of the secular life-world is the sole condition for a reinvigoration, as it is the criterion for a reassessment, of the Catholic tradition and the Catholic liturgy.

# *Notes*

## CHAPTER I

1. See Garry Wills's ironic notation that just when she had finally "made it," Catholicism proceeded to commit *harikiri!* Wills, *Bare Ruined Choirs* (Garden City, N.Y.: Doubleday, 1972), pp. 1ff.

2. See Wills's description in *Bare Ruined Choirs*, chapter 1; James Hitchcock, *The Decline and Fall of Radical Catholicism* (Garden City, N.Y.: Doubleday Image, 1972), chapters 1, 3, and 5; and also Andrew Greeley, *The New Agenda* (Garden City, N.Y.: Doubleday, 1973), p. 13.

3. See the John Mannion article, "The Making of a Dissident," *Commonweal* 97, no. 15 (January 19, 1973), pp. 344–46.

4. "No one can predict with any certainty that the church will have a visible existence by the end of the century." Hitchcock, *Decline and Fall*, p. 23.

5. We are here borrowing a concept of praxis or "critical reflection" generated most specifically in the Frankfurter Schule. This concept is a theoretical understanding of social change whose purpose is creative action within social change. The similarity of this concept to John Dewey's instrumentalism is interesting; however, both in our use of it and in that of the Frankfort School there is, I believe, more of an emphasis on a stable theory (or system of symbols) through which change is understood and hypotheses for action are developed. See Martin Jay, *The Dialectical Imagination* (Boston: Little, Brown and Co., 1973), especially chapter 2, and Jürgen Habermas, *Theorie und Praxis* (Neuwied and Berlin: Luchterhand, 1963).

6. Perhaps a better model, then, for interpreting the crisis of

Catholicism than the model of a fallen Imperial Rome is that of the covenant people forced by the prophets and by the changes of their history to look for and acknowledge a *new* form of the covenant because the old had been destroyed and made useless. See the creative interpretation of this prophetic role in Gerhard Von Rad, *Old Testament Theology*, tr. D. M. G. Stalker (New York: Harper and Row, 1962), especially vol. 2, part 2.

7. It is interesting that possibly the two most stimulating and creative current Catholic books of theology accept this basic principle but give it a slightly different referent than the present work. I refer to Johannes B. Metz, *Theology of the World*, tr. William Glen-Doepel (New York: Herder and Herder, 1969), and Gustavo Gutiérrez, *A Theology of Liberation*, tr. Sister Caridad Inda and John Eagleson (Maryknoll, N.Y.: Orbis Books, 1973). In both of these works, the classical task of the church in the world, its ethic, is radically revised into a socially "liberating" ethic in the light not only of our interpretation of the biblical and traditional sources but also of the needs and aspirations of modern man.

8. See Greeley, *New Agenda*, foreword, p. 32.

9. For a more thorough discussion of these problems, compare the author's *Naming the Whirlwind* (Indianapolis: Bobbs-Merrill, 1969), part 1, chapters 1–4, 6, and *Religion and the Scientific Future* (New York: Harper and Row, 1970), chapter 1.

10. For a full discussion of the present problems of the Protestant churches, especially in America, see the author's *How the Church Can Minister to the World Without Losing Itself* (New York: Harper and Row, 1964).

11. In saying that in the present Protestantism has lost and probably in the near future will lose some of its creativity, I do not mean to imply that Protestantism essentially represents a less creative or authentic form of Christianity. In the last two hundred years it has been more creative than has Catholicism; and in the future, in a different historical situation, it may well again achieve a greater creativity and authenticity.

12. Admittedly this symbol (the mystical Body of Christ) is only *one* of the traditional symbols of the church in Catholic history. (Note, for example, the effort of Vatican II to replace or at least to supplement this symbol by that of the people of God.) However, my point, which is by no means incontestable, is that this is the *most* significant and determinative symbol, besides that of its complementary symbol, the continuation of the Incarnation. For the church was conceived in terms of the symbol of the Body of

Christ in the Western Catholic tradition from Cyprian and Augustine onward.

13. See the discussion, long before Vatican II, of Catholic *caritas* and its probable sources in the author's *Shantung Compound* (New York: Harper and Row, 1966), chapter 9.

14. The increasing participation of Catholics, both lay and clerical, in active movements of social protest and reform has been evident for some years in this country, represented by such outstanding names as James Groppi and Philip and Daniel Berrigan. In South America this participation in more radical form is even more significant and effective, reflectively represented in the powerful theology of social liberation of Father Gutiérrez.

15. This is the main thesis of James Hitchcock's castigation of both liberals and radicals: that in removing these traditional structures of Catholic life, with all their admitted anachronisms and often absurd trivia, they have removed as well the sacramental communion with the sacred on which Catholicism, and probably all religion, ultimately depends. That the creative continuation of Catholicism may well depend rather on the *opposite* assertion, Hitchcock seems implicitly to recognize when he admits throughout his account that this old, traditional structure of authority and life was no longer able to communicate the holy to Catholic people and was, in fact, dead or about to die. See Hitchcock, *Decline and Fall*, pp. 38–40, 78–79, 133. See also Wills, *Bare Ruined Choirs*, pp. 8–11 and chapter 13; and Greeley, *New Agenda*, p. 2.

16. Karl Rahner insists the tradition *cannot* remain static, caught in past formulations that are given an absolute, transhistorical status, lest all theology cease to have any meaning. *Theological Investigations* (Baltimore: Helicon Press, 1961), vol. 1, chapter 1.

17. The two aspects of modernity that Catholic modernism sought valiantly to include within a new interpretation of Catholicism were: the principle of the relativity of all cultural, and so all conceptual, forms; and the principle of the participation of the autonomous mind and conscience in all that is true and good for the conscience. To encompass both principles, the ill-starred "method of immanence" was projected by Blondel and Édouard Le Roy in opposition to the extrinsicism of the tradition.

18. See Andrew Greeley's comment, *New Agenda*, chapter 1, on the trivial and defensive character of recent Catholic thought. There were, of course, vivid exceptions in the nineteenth and early twentieth centuries to this evaluation that was perhaps too critical. The exceptions include Möhler, Newman, Blondel, Le Roy, Tyrrel, Von

Hugel, Karl Adam, Gilson, and Maritain, to name only a few. These are great figures. It may be a faulty and even prejudiced judgment, but it does not seem to me that even this tradition of thought represents as free, creative, and profound a tradition as does the Protestant tradition contemporary with it. The reasons for this restriction of thought seem to lie in the dogmatic control on fundamental issues, the consequent avoidance of basic theological themes, and the slowly actualized alienation of the Catholic mind from its cultural environment, which we are here trying to describe.

19. In this description of the "problems" that culture sets for the church, we have omitted the question of the mission and task of the church in the world. Clearly, different cultural and historical situations create different problems for praxis, the activity of the church in transforming the world (and the church). A feudal culture, an oppressed culture (oppressed from the outside or the inside), an economically unjust culture, a racist culture, a corrupted democratic culture, an exploitative capitalistic culture, a Communist culture—each calls for a different form of Christian praxis, a unique interpretation of the call to liberate, heal, secure, and redeem the world. This relation of the church to its contemporary culture is taken as central by both Metz and Gutiérrez. We agree that it is central. However, as we argue here, in our own situation at least (and this is *the* guiding principle for Gutiérrez on this point [*Theology of Liberation*, p. 14]), the questions of ecclesiology are also pressing and significant. These questions include that of how the church is to understand itself: its authority, hierarchy, dogma, law, sacrament, and life style in the light of both the changes in its history and the present secular character of the cultural environment. For if there is no authentic and credible Catholic community, how can that community reorient itself to the world in order to liberate the world? Perhaps wrongly, I believe the question of secularity, as opposed to that of oppressive domination, has not yet appeared in South America as pointedly as it has here.

20. Presumably it is to this group that Hitchcock refers in *Decline and Fall* when he uses the word "radicals," although he makes no clear distinction between their attitudes and those of the "liberals." He regards the liberal desire to modernize traditional forms as the beginning of a slide into the radical indifference to anything at all religious. Part of the effort of the present analysis is to distinguish two quite different responses to modern culture and its secularity. The difference between the liberal and radical, so defined, is

not, as with Hitchcock, confused into one response. His view not only fails to describe faithfully the present situation, and therefore fails to explain that situation; it also reflects an attitude of utter despair for the future. Hitchcock admits freely throughout his book that the traditional forms had already lost their religious and moral authority and power, thus by implication rendering the conservative position useless. He goes on to identify in his analysis liberal attempts to reform the church with the radical indifference to religion of all sorts. Thus he appears to envision no useful and hopeful option for the church at all. In the end he despairs entirely, it would seem, of the divine promise to the church on which his own conservative position has always been founded.

21. It is interesting to note that a careful study from the vantage point of the Catholic modernists reveals how close they were in essentials to this "conservative" position. They asserted the principles of the relativity of doctrine and the unworkability of extrinsicism in dogma, doctrine, law, and practice. Nevertheless, it is plain that supernaturalistic and absolutist principles of authority remained in their views of dogma, magisterium, and canon law.

22. Any visit to a Catholic campus or any talk with students in a Catholic seminary verifies this observation. At first the questions will range somewhat as follows: how can we reinterpret our Catholic belief, our Catholic habits, our Catholic identity so as to exist in harmony with modernity? But then, sooner or later, the more ultimate question always appears: why should we be Catholics or Christians at all, and not just humanistic and secular? This same shift from the reinterpretation of a religious identity that was substantial, taken for granted, to a personal identity that could be, and perhaps had already become, secular and naturalistic, took place in Protestant groups and at Protestant colleges in the twenties and thirties. Possibly very soon Catholic life will "catch up" to ours, but at present the two levels are inextricably confused and confusing.

## CHAPTER III

1. See Karl Rahner's clear preference for the "biblical" view of deity in "Theos in the New Testament," in *Theological Investigations* (Baltimore: Helican Press, 1961), vol. 1, pp. 79–148, and the

sudden appearance of "process" philosophy and eschatological theologies to replace traditional Thomistic categories in almost all Roman Catholic circles.

2. This is the character of A. N. Whitehead's own view of God, though many of his interpreters (especially Charles Hartshorne, William Christian, and John Cobb) seek for the reasons here given to make the process God more "ultimate" than this.

3. Even if theology is viewed as not so much incarnational as eschatological, still this aspect of narrative language is implied; only then, instead of centering theological language on a story about the *past*, we center theological language on the divine promises for the *future*, and our words describe the "new" in the historical future and the God who is to bring that "new" about. In both cases there is essentially included a historical referent for theological language.

4. We use this phrase to guard against the common misapprehension that a philosophy that understands *all* events to be particular or unique may still not be able to encompass and express the uniqueness implied in this point. The uniqueness involved in all events and in every human person is *not* the same as the uniqueness claimed by traditional Christianity for its founder as the unique and irreplaceable locus of special divine activity, as the central and ultimate *Kairos* of a history made up of unique particulars.

5. See Whitehead's description of a metaphysical category: "Speculative philosophy is the endeavor to frame a coherent, logical, necessary, system of general ideas in terms of which every element of our experience can be interpreted." "The metaphysical first principles can never fail of exemplification. We can never catch the actual world taking a holiday from their sway." A. N. Whitehead, *Process and Reality* (New York: The Macmillan Company, 1929), pp. 4 and 7.

6. The strong criticism of this type of theological language vis-à-vis God found in Hegel and Schleiermacher, Tillich and the process theologians shows that "biblical theology" so described is neither the exclusive nor even the normative form of Protestant theology; it also shows that the neo-orthodox rejection of philosophical and scientific analysis as intrinsic to theology is not characteristic of Protestantism as such. There may in fact be an "essential nature" characteristic of all Protestant theology, but certainly historically it cannot be defined in terms exclusively of either reformation or neo-Reformation theology.

7. The reference is to Van A. Harvey's excellent discussion of the

"morality of historical knowledge" and its requirements for an honest theologian; see Van A. Harvey, *The Historian and the Believer* (New York; The Macmillan Company, 1966), chapter 4.

CHAPTER IV

1. No better example of this modern "prejudice" against the past and almost blanket approval of the future can be found than the definition of sin in much modern theology as "bondage to the past" and of salvation and freedom as "openness to the future." This strange understanding of sin as "pastness" and of salvation as "futurity" has dominated all three of modern Protestant theology's otherwise quite diverse modes: it was characteristic of liberal theology's view that sin arose from our carnal, animal inheritance, which would gradually be dissolved by a progressive historical movement towards the future Kingdom. It reappeared in Heideggerian dress in Bultmann's understanding of sin, to which we have here referred. And now it characterizes most contemporary eschatological or futuristic theology (see especially the writings of Jürgen Moltmann), where past and present are described as desolate, godless and unjust, and the future as the only realm of God's saving "new." From this strange agreement about tradition and the future between utterly diverse theologies one might conclude that the invariable factor in this important issue stems neither from Christian experience nor the biblical word—which each of these three theological views interpreted in radically different ways—but rather that it stems from the modern secular "tradition" of a progressive time sequence derived from the eighteenth and nineteenth centuries, and subsequently incorporated in widely different ways into contemporary Christian theology.

2. No contemporary philosopher has better illustrated this dialectic of the need for tradition within a history always capable of the new than has Whitehead; and, interestingly, considering the vast differences in their points of view, no theologian has better embodied this same dialectic than Wolfhart Pannenberg.

3. See the author's *Naming the Whirlwind*, part 1, chapters 2, 3, and 6, part 2, chapters 2, 3, and 4.

4. The history of doctrine or theology represents, to be sure, a

continual reinterpretation of the primary biblical symbols. However, the reverse is also true: the history of exegesis is itself a function of the history of theology. This can be shown by comparing the exegesis of the *Letter to the Romans* by Augustine, Thomas, Luther, Calvin, Wesley, a "modernist," and Barth, and finding in the exegesis itself almost all the significant continuities and changes that would need to be elaborated in an adequate history of doctrine.

5. See Gerhard Von Rad, *Old Testament Theology*, tr. D. M. G. Stalker (New York: Harper and Row, 1962), vol. 1, pp. 105 ff., and Wolfhart Pannenberg, *Basic Questions in Theology*, tr. George H. Kehm (Philadelphia: Fortress Press, 1970), vol. 1, pp. 6 ff.

6. See the author's effort to reconceive the doctrine of creation in *Maker of Heaven and Earth* (New York: Doubleday, 1959).

## CHAPTER V

1. This emphasis on process and eschatological theology currently dominates Catholic as well as Protestant theology. For an analysis of contemporary Catholic theology from this point of view (and perhaps overstating his case), see George A. Lindbeck, *The Future of Roman Catholic Theology* (Philadelphia: Fortress Press, 1970).

2. Hence the relevance for even the Marxist Ernst Bloch of Christian symbolism. As he clearly sees, and as I have argued in the text, Christian symbolism points those who live within it to the future, to the not-yet, to what might be: it is messianic, identifying the perfection of man and of history with a future utopia and thus implying and even demanding creative changes in the present. Thus for Bloch Christianity (to be sure a Christianity without God) is the fulfillment of religion insofar as it holds before us in the present the sacredness and mysterious depth of man, the possibility of a better future, a Kingdom of love and righteousness to come. See Ernst Bloch, *Das Princip Hoffnung* (Frankfurt: Suhrkamp Verlag, 1959), vol. 3, pp. 1323–33, 1450–64, 1482–1628; or *Man on His Own*, tr. E. B. Ashton (New York: Herder and Herder, 1970).

3. For another powerful vindication of this critique, this time from within the orbit of Western social science, see Alvin Gouldner, *The Coming Crisis of Western Sociology* (Equinox Books, 1971),

and Gibson Winter, *Elements for a Social Ethic* (New York: The Macmillan Company, 1966), especially chapter 2.

4. See Gouldner's convincing demonstration that much of current empirical sociology, especially the functional analysis of the Parsonian school, is an "ideology" because it has as its own basis the distinguished status and the professional needs and worries of the sociologist himself in present-day academic, capitalistic, and "welfare" society. Gouldner, *The Coming Crisis.*

5. Herbert Marcuse, *One Dimensional Man* (London: Sphere Books, 1968), chapter 6.

6. See as the prime example, B. F. Skinner, *Beyond Freedom and Dignity.* For an explicit assertion of this methodological determinism in a "scientific" study of man in society, see the cultural evolutionist Julian H. Steward: "I emphasise causality because any assumption that teleological or orthogenetic principles, divine intervention or free will are at work will nullify scientific explanation. To those who disagree I can only say that science must proceed *as if* natural laws operate consistently and without exception, as if all cultures and all aspects of human behaviour had determinants—no matter how difficult the task of unraveling the intricately interrelated phenomena." "Cultural Evolution Today" in *Changing Man,* eds. K. Haselden and P. Hefner (New York: Doubleday, 1967), pp. 50–51.

## CHAPTER VII

1. The contemporary phenomena of pentecostal experiences ("speaking with tongues") seems to belie these remarks about modernity. For groups devoted to a firm sense of these sorts of workings of the Spirit flourish in many of our churches, Protestant and Catholic alike. Perhaps such groups show the dissolution of modernity as "secular" in the sense here described, as quite possibly the counterculture also does. My guess is that they do not. Rather it seems to me that such groups are only *partly* dominated spiritually by modernity (as are fundamentalist Protestants) and that the eagerness with which they embrace "the Spirit" in these forms shows how divested of ultimacy and sacrality the rest of their world is. The usual response of their pastor or priest (of incomprehension, grudging admiration, and helplessness) is the best sign (or consequence)

of what I mean by "secularity" and so modernity. His objection is not that these "speakers" are not orthodox Catholic in their piety, but that as a modern man he simply cannot credit, or understand, or participate in these experiences—though he can hardly deny their power.

2. This problem is in this sense similar to that of God-language. It is important that old, anachronistic forms of theological discourse be abandoned simply because they have become meaningless and irrelevant to us; but the introduction of new forms does not in itself guarantee the ability to speak meaningfully about God. It is, as it were, a necessary but not a sufficient condition, the deeper issue again being a sense of the holy or sacred as the prior condition for the meaningfulness of *any* form of theology.

3. As is evident, these statements imply that to me the mystical mode is a special vocation or gift within the Christian community and not normative for it. For most of us God comes to us through finite media and not directly, that is, *in* life and history and not beyond them. This appearance of the divine in and through the creaturely and the historical seems to me normative for the Christian tradition and for its main forms of worship. Here I seem to be in some disagreement with Louis Dupré (see his interesting book *The Other Dimension* [Garden City: Doubleday, 1972], especially chapter 12).

4. For this reason, as the history of religion illustrates, *any* creature can become a vehicle for some revelation of the holy, and in turn revelation of some sort may be said to be universal in scope. Obviously many of the differences between religions stem from the vast differences in the media that are taken as essential clues to the divine that is present in all creatures.

5. This is only one of the bases for the presence of Word as well as sacrament in Christian existence; others will appear subsequently in this chapter.

6. Generally discussions of "legitimate" worship have approached this interrelationship from the other side, namely, by asking: "What forms of worship are in fact 'genuine expressions' of Jesus Christ?"—that is to say, by asking for "valid" forms of sacrament and word. Since I think that this question, while important, is not the most helpful clue to our present problems of worship, but rather that the relations of even "valid" forms to ordinary, secular experience is the heart of the problem, we shall attack this difficult fortress, so to speak, from the rear, and explore the modes of the appearance of the holy in ordinary experience.

7. For a fuller discussion of the dependence of all levels of our "nature" on the presence of the divine ultimacy, and the character of our "awareness" in ordinary life of this dimension of our existence, cf. the author's *Naming the Whirlwind, the Renewal of God-Language* (Indianapolis: Bobbs-Merrill, 1969), part 2, chapters 3 and 4.

8. A defense of this "Augustinian" viewpoint on knowledge and truth in terms of modern scientific inquiry is found in the author's *Religion and the Scientific Future* (New York: Harper and Row, 1970), chapter 2.